Cave Refectory Road

Ian Adams is a writer, mentor and artist. A popular Greenbelt festival speaker, he is author of the daily Morning Bell call to prayer in the monastic tradition. He's an Anglican priest, and was co-founder and abbot of the experimental mayBe community in Oxford. Ian is a director of Stillpoint, a project seeking to nurture spiritual practice, and a partner in the see:change project encouraging personal and community development.

Cave Refectory Road

monastic rhythms for contemporary living

Ian Adams

LITURGICAL PRESS

Collegeville, Minnesota

www.litpress.org

Published for the United States and Canada by
LITURGICAL PRESS
Collegeville, Minnesota 56321

Copyright © Ian Adams 2010

Originally published in the UK under the title
Cave Refectory Road
by the Canterbury Press of
13-17 Long Lane, London EC1A 9PN

1   2   3   4   5   6   7   8   9

Library of Congress Cataloging-in-Publication Data

Adams, Ian.
    Cave Refectory Road : monastic rhythms for contemporary living /
Ian Adams.
        p.   cm.
    Originally published: London : Canterbury Press Norwich, 2010.
    Includes bibliographical references.
    ISBN 978-0-8146-3444-8 — ISBN 978-0-8146-3445-5 (ebook)
    1. Spiritual life—Christianity.   2. Monastic and religious life.   I. Title.
BV4501.3.A3325   2012
248.4—dc23   2012007796

contents

v

1

reshaping the world – bringing monastic practice, wisdom and spirituality into everyday life

What does it take
to mark the canvas
to write the line
to play the chord
to plough the field
to cross the river
to change the world?

Perhaps
the courage
to let become
what is waiting to become

    Ian Adams, 'What does it take?'

Who will give the best of their creative gifts so that suffering throughout the world may be alleviated?

    Brother Roger, *The Sources of Taizé*

disillusionment and hope

Late one evening in early summer, the end of a long day travelling. I'm at the edge of the causeway that leads to the Holy Island of Lindisfarne off the coast of north east England. I get out of the car and look across at the island. I've been looking forward for a long time to this moment, sensing that St Aidan and the monastic way of life that he pioneered in this part of Northumbria might be important to me. Twice a day the tides sweep in from the North Sea over the sands to cover the causeway. There's an incoming tide but still time to cross. I hesitate, a strange pause after so much anticipation. What might this require of me? What might it do to me? And how might it make some kind of difference for good in my world?

In the United Kingdom in the election year of 2010 there has been much attention given to the idea that the country is broken. There is plenty of evidence to suggest that we are at the very least a damaged society, if not a broken one. But there are also optimistic voices pointing out what is still good, suggesting the possibility of re-making what is broken and highlighting the streams and stories of extraordinary wonder that dance with light through our ordinary lives. This book seeks to be another optimistic voice, imagining how the traditional monastic way may help to bring about something truly hopeful for the world – a new flowering of personal and community life in the twenty-first century.

This book tries to understand how monasticism has evolved and taken specific shape among followers of the enigmatic first-century Jewish teacher Jesus of Nazareth. It asks if it might be possible to take monastic practice, wisdom and spirituality into everyday life, and tries to imagine what that might look like in both personal and community settings. It wonders how a renewed exploration of the monastic way in the context of daily life might contribute to a reshaping of the wider world for the good of all, replacing our widespread sense of disillusionment with hope.

There seems to be something compelling about the monastic way. Whenever I talk about monastic spirituality with individuals or groups, there is always someone who seems to light up. Attention deepens, and there's a shift to the seat edge; as if a long-forgotten, ancient bell is tolling deep within them. This interest is not just cerebral or pragmatic. It seems to come from something that they cannot quite name but is palpable all the same, as if they are unknowing carriers of some memory of a monastic life, and our shared conversation is awakening that dream.

In suggesting this I'm aware of the possibility of romanticizing the monastic way of life. I hope that this book does not do that. The monastic life is a rigorous calling, and the kind of engagement that I am suggesting for those of us in 'regular life'[1] will be demanding as well as freeing. Please note that I use the term 'regular life' here simply as shorthand for the way that most of us live, with the usual variety and mix of jobs and commitments, anxieties and celebrations, friends and families. No life is 'just' regular; every life is extraordinary, every life unique.

peering over the wall

Whatever we do in life our motives are usually mixed – and the motives for entering the religious life have always been fantastically varied. Love, devotion, calling, desperation, obligation, poverty, scandal and war have all played their part. My own motives for exploring the monastic way include a few, though thankfully not all, of the above. I'm not a monk or friar, at least not in the 'real', vow-committed sense. I'm peering over the wall, and nurturing friendships. I'm playing the songs and copying the steps. I'm scrumping apples in the monastery orchard. And I'm discovering something in this ancient way of life that is helping me – and perhaps may prove to be a gift to others too. I sense that there's a deep stream of possibility in the monastic way that can help us in the twenty-first century to find new ways to live – in balance with ourselves, reconnected to our fellow humanity, in harmony with the planet and at ease with Mystery. Whatever emerges may also enable Christianity to become once again a source of goodness in and for the world.

This book, of course, emerges from a certain context. I have been for many years a would-be follower of the teacher/ storyteller/healer/prophet Jesus. This is my setting. I have found a place of belonging in the community called 'the Church' and the way of life called 'Christianity' that has, for better (sometimes, compellingly) or worse (often, infuriatingly) grown up in the name of this Jesus. My own following in his way has often been ragged and ambiguous, riddled with inconsistencies, a continual tussle between love and its many opposites. But I keep coming back this way. He holds my attention.

In the six years prior to writing this book I was co-founder and later abbot of mayBe – an experimental and evolving Anglican (that is Church of England) community in Oxford – which has found the monastic stream to be a rich resource for life and mission. I refer to mayBe's story and experience in a number of places in the book, and I'm so grateful to the people of mayBe community for their generous and life-enhancing company. I am also drawing from the monastic source in a current role facilitating the growth of a number of diverse missional communities in the UK. This book reflects on all these experiences, and also draws on the stories of other emerging projects and communities around the world. Most importantly, it works with original source material from what we might refer to as 'real monasticism'. The Desert Fathers and Mothers, St Benedict's Rule and Francis of Assisi all make appearances, as do some wonderful contemporary expressions of the religious life – notably the ecumenical (that is with participants not confined to one denomination) communities at Taizé in France and Bose in Italy.

My hope is that this book may be of inspiration not only to those who see themselves as being somewhere in the Jesus tradition of faith, but also that it may inspire people of other faith traditions or none – anyone who wants to see our scarred and shining world become all the good that it can become. My instinct is that the life, teachings and presence of Jesus (called the Christ – the truly Special One) can be a gift to all people, in all places, at all times – and that the story of the monastic way as worked at and lived out over the centuries in the Jesus tradition is full of wisdom and possibility for all people.

I am particularly interested in three connected aspects of the monastic way. The first is the *devotion* that characterizes the monastic search for God. The second is the monastic conviction that this search, while always personal, is often best ventured in *community*. The third is the possibility that the monastic life, which on the surface might appear introspective, can in fact bring astonishing *change for good* to wider society.

seeing clearly

I want to make clear that this book is in no way a valedictory for the traditional monastic life. Despite the challenges facing many monastic communities, it's my conviction that at this time, more than ever, we need people to take the tough path of the formal religious life. We need their pioneering, their example, their experience. We need their attention, their purity, their devotion. And I am confident that some imaginative and courageous people will continue to take this route as long as humans are around on this fragile but beautiful planet. May it be so.

Occasionally in the book I use the word *mission* or *missional*. When I speak about mission I am imagining people learning together to become fully human in the spirit and the way of the teacher Jesus – and so becoming a gift to our world. I am imagining individuals and communities becoming fully present to both the toughness and wonder of existence. I am imagining people in serving engagement with the communities around us, helping the goodness present in all things to flourish. I am imagining God's dynamic dance of love and life – the missio Dei (the mission *of* God, the mission *is* God's) – flowing in and around all that exists.

This is a flow that can be entered, a stream that can be stepped into, a continual reorientation of purpose and practice. To enter this flow is to begin to follow in the way of Jesus, aspiring to become (in the words of the gospel writer Matthew) what Jesus called 'disciples'. It involves learning to see what is real, learning not to control, learning to give and learning to wait. It becomes in time a way of life, a way of being. Authentic mission starts its work with us. The world cannot be transformed if we are not transformed.

In this book I sometimes use the phrase *religious life*. The life of monks and nuns is not always restricted to a monastic settlement, enclosure, convent or monastery. As we shall see in Chapter 5, some orders – notably friars – live much of their life in the open, on the road, away from the community house, and some live in solitude as hermits. I use the wider term *religious life* from time to time to remind us of this breadth of the monastic stream, and the word *religious* to refer to the wide variety of monastics, whether living alone as hermits, enclosed in a settlement of some sort, or out in the wider world.

live a story of community

There is much in this book about how we can engage with the religious life in a personal way, as individuals. But there is equally a focus on the shaping of community life, and how this can, when lived with openness and commitment, become a natural rhythm of mission serving the wider world. The late Br Roger of the monastic community at Taizé in the Burgundy region of France urges us to 'live a parable of community' (Roger, p. 49).

This simple-sounding idea can be taken as a summary of his understanding of the gospel (the 'good news story') of Jesus as prayed, pondered and practised by the monastics over the centuries. In the teaching tradition of Jesus a parable is a story that provokes and teases, sparking questions and offering insights. The parable as story has the capacity to bring change for good in the hearer – but it also offers itself up for rejection. The choice belongs to the hearer. So for Br Roger the monastic way comes down in its simplest form to this, a stunning mix of simplicity and challenge. Live a story of community, a story that will spark off a festival of stories, a conversation that will release a flood of conversations, a picture that will inspire a gallery of pictures, every story, every conversation, every picture bringing hope, carrying good, re-making the world – as taught and lived by the teacher Jesus.

Ever since Roger and the brothers began to devote themselves to this task, people have come in large numbers to Taizé to participate in what has emerged – thousands of people, each year, and astonishingly a majority of these are young adults, the very age group apparently least attracted to conventional religion. Something powerful seems to happen when, in the spirit of the monastics, people begin to experience the way of community as taught and modelled by Jesus.

'Happy the community', continues Br Roger, 'that has become an abyss of kindness: it lets Christ shine through, incomparably' (Roger, p. 67). That's an astonishing partnering of nouns – abyss and kindness. Fall into this, Br Roger seems to be saying, and nothing will ever be the same again. The light of the world will shine wherever you are, whatever the setting, whatever your circumstances. A community that begins to follow the Christ as imagined and taught by him with any measure of authenticity cannot help but share the light and life of God. And so community life becomes, with great simplicity and humility, a mission of service to the world.

Ever wanted to change the world? Live a story of community, suggest the monastics, and that change might just begin.

Note

1 Ironically, to describe 'normal life' as 'regular life' is the very opposite of the monastic understanding. For the monastics, the word regular derives from *regula* or rule, and refers to a life lived under a rule. I'm grateful to Abbot Stuart Burns OSB for this insight. It might therefore be more accurate to refer to our everyday life as 'irregular'!

2

ancient paths, emerging patterns – exploring monastic practices of cave, refectory and road

Look, wild geese
a sign for us
there are five
no six, seven you say

they take to the wind
as we come near
wild, of course,
they fly west
dancing the edge of light
in ancient joyful stream

Ian Adams, 'Look wild geese'

Our life is a faint tracing on the surface of mystery.

Annie Dillard, *Pilgrim at Tinker Creek*

jazz monastics: tradition and improvisation

The jazz record *Kind of Blue* by Miles Davis is a constant companion of mine. It's a piece of music that seems to have the power to give new colour, shape or possibility to the day. It takes some old ingredients, and does something with them that I can only describe as miraculous. The practice of improvisational jazz may be a really helpful way of thinking about how we engage with a living tradition as ancient as that of monasticism.

One of the vital ingredients for creating great jazz music is a consciousness of, and a love for, the tradition. *Kind of Blue* was hugely innovative when it was created by Miles Davis and friends in 1959, but it was still jazz. It carried the long-told stories, the well-crafted forms and the much-loved spirit of the tradition from which it emerged and to which it gave itself. The music would not be here were it not for all the musicians and players who have gone before. But if jazz reminds us of our traditions, it also calls us into improvisation. Each track on *Kind of Blue* begins with a theme – but then moves in unexpected directions. New sound-paths open up that are still true to the theme, still faithful to the spirit of the piece, but releasing the music to fly higher and further, to go to places that it may not have been before. And the fluidity of the music seems to ask of the hearer: '… so what line will you play?'

Something interesting may happen when we learn to hear the monastic mothers and fathers – like Anthony of Egypt, Benedict of Nursia, Hilda of Whitby and Theresa of Avila – as great exponents of the jazz of religious life. It will surely inspire us to love their tradition, but it may also encourage us to make our own improvisation around their great themes. In Matthew's Gospel (13.52) Jesus talks of the scribes – the interpreters of the Law – as being 'like the master of a household who brings out of his treasure what is new and what is old'. The new flourishes out of what has gone before. The old cannot help but inspire new interpretations beyond the imagining of the original players. We need the learning, wisdom and practice of those who have played the music before us. In becoming familiar with their rhythms, patterns and pauses we may find the freedom to let the jazz of the devotional life take surprising new shape.

Human life is a tender and mysterious happening, a thing of troubling wonder, what Annie Dillard memorably refers to as a 'faint tracing on the surface of mystery' (Dillard, p. 9). This fragile and brilliant existence frequently calls us to open ourselves to a world that is beyond our control or comprehension. There is much to be said for engaging with this unpredictable life in the light and company of the wise and curious who have come this way before us, and so become new players of the jazz of the religious life.

cave. refectory. road.

Running through this book are three related but distinct paths (or we might say, *tracks*, in the spirit of jazz) in the traditional monastic life. Each has particular wisdom for the twenty-first-century person. Each offers insights for creating community. Each may inspire an emerging Christianity for our time that is good for the wider world.

The first I'm referring to as **the cave.**

'Like a fish going towards the sea,' said St Anthony, 3rd and 4th century 'father of monks', 'we must hurry to reach our cell, for fear that if we delay outside we will lose our interior watchfulness.'

Benedicta Ward, *The Sayings of the Desert Fathers*, p. 3

The cave is the symbol of a life of withdrawal, as practised by those we might reasonably identify as the first Christian monastics, the so-called Desert Fathers and Mothers. Initially in personal solitude, then banding together in proto-monasteries, and continued to this day by monastic communities who have chosen to locate themselves in remote and challenging settings. The type of community that first emerged here was shaped in a tough wilderness life of stillness and contemplation, of survival amidst the elements and battle with the powers of darkness.

This is life rooted in stillness, prayer and simplicity, practised by people of the desert, of the cell, of the cave. This is the deep bedrock, down to which, I will suggest, any committed spiritual traveller and any serious form of the movement dedicated to following in the way of the Christ, must go. This is the starting point, the vital story of reconnection with self and with whoever or whatever we may think of as God, the Other or the Mystery. There is no shortcut and no more palatable way. This is the place of self-revelation and the site of God-encounter. The cave is essential.

The second path I'm referring to as **the refectory** – a monastic term for the canteen, dining room or eating place:

> 'In whatever place you live' – St Anthony again – 'do not easily leave it.'
> Ward, p. 2

Sign of stability, hospitality and presence, the refectory is symbolic of monastic community committed to a place, made real in long-term commitments and epitomized perhaps by community buildings. So imagine the monastic house, in the early centuries built simply from sand and reeds or wattle and daub, later of wood and slate or brick and tile, eventually – and now familiar to us – in buildings of stone and glass, bathed in light and shadow. The type of community that emerges here keeps the cave-pattern of prayer, stillness and study of the scriptures, but settles into local rhythms of life, growing food, engaging with the local population, becoming a resource in all kinds of ways for the surrounding community.

This is religious life firmly located in a particular place, with the life of the community shaped by and offered out from the chapel, the cloister, the library, the infirmary and the refectory. This path we can imagine encouraging us to be committed to our neighbourhoods, offering life to all-comers. This is a story of reconnection with community and with lived place. Like the cave, this too is essential, a place of earth-rootedness and community-connection.

The third path I'm calling **the road**.

> 'Our life and death', says St Anthony, 'is with our neighbour'.
> Ward, p. 3

This is religious life lived in the open, in the market place, on the street. This path was pioneered by some of the earliest monks who set out not knowing where they were going – the so-called Celtic monks of the Dark Ages, and later in the early Middle Ages by the various orders of friars – notably the Franciscans, the Friars Minor, who Francis referred to as 'pilgrims and exiles',[1] and the Dominicans, the order of preachers. Still based on a rhythm of prayer, this is community shaped by engagement with people wherever they are encountered, springing from a belief that God is already at work in the world.

This encourages us to live in the public sphere, to be shaped by contact with neighbour and stranger, recognizing that the journey is as important as the destination, open to encounter, travelling light. This is a story of reconnection with people and common space. Again, like the cave and the refectory, the road in some form seems essential – a place of continual discovery and world-engagement.

Cave, refectory, road. Each of these emphases in the religious life is linked – hence the quotation in each case from St Anthony. And each can be seen in the practice and teaching of the rabbi (a Jewish term for a religious teacher) Jesus as seen in the Gospels. The *cave* can be seen in his going to the desert or to the mountain, to reorientate himself, to find restoration, to pray. The *refectory* in the life of Jesus can be seen both in his commitment to synagogue and temple – places of stability and hope, ritual and learning for his people – and in his practice of creating community around a table. And the *road* is perhaps his most easily identified practice of connection and community – the travelling band of rabbi and followers, healing, teaching, questioning, sharing meals as they go.

Each of these paths has the potential to bring about change in us for good in an age of dislocation, upheaval and uncertainty. Each may shape an emerging Christianity in the twenty-first century, helping to bring about the kind of better world that Jesus described when he spoke of the 'kingdom of heaven' coming near.

an authentic life

There's something about the monastic stream that makes its learning and experience particularly important at this time in the human story – a quest for authenticity. It's a commonly held thesis that one of the identifiers of the globalized postmodern (or post-postmodern) society that we find ourselves in is the ability for us to construct an identity for ourselves. This can of course be very powerful and freedom-bringing. But perhaps inevitably there's a certain shallowness to the whole thing, even when it is ironic and knowing. In this context the apparent authenticity of the monastic way has a real appeal. There's an almost deliberate cultivation of the opposite of cool. At the surface-level, in the religious communities that I know, sandals with socks are more than fine. But of course there's something deeper than an anti-fashion statement running through the monastic way. This is the search for authenticity, and is actually the antithesis of trying to be relevant. The monastics are what they are, and who they are. Their idea is not to find a shape that will please, attract or draw admiration. The point is to seek after God in a wholehearted way, with love, simplicity and devotion. If you are tired of pastiche, parody and the cult of celebrity, this represents an exhilarating return to the garden of our beginnings.

Now of course we can idealize the monastic way, and no doubt within religious communities there remains the temptation to cultivate identities. But from the time of the earliest monastic communities in the desert a commitment to authenticity has been prized. This is a tapping into something ancient. And the idea of an authentic and ancient monasticism, rediscovered and re-expressed in the now, is full of possibility if we are looking for ways to reshape the world for good.

I am going to suggest ten particular ways in which the ancient religious life – at the cave, in the refectory and on the road – may shape a renewed way of being truly human in and for the world. Each chapter concludes with a simple way to begin taking monastic wisdom and practice into everyday life. Some of these ideas are already being practised by individuals and groups, communities and projects around the world; others are perhaps yet to be explored.

Time to go to the cave.

Note

1 The Rule of St Francis, ch. 6 (see www.friar.org/).

3

to the cave – monastic patterns of withdrawal and prayer opening up space for encounter beyond our experience

a loft, an opening
room to breathe
into stillness

a window, light streams
hard lines soften
possibilities emerge

a cell, a look-out post
to look within
and a shuffling of priorities

       Ian Adams, 'St Ives'

The beginning of the good news of Jesus Christ, the Son of God.
As it is written in the prophet Isaiah, 'See, I am sending my messenger
ahead of you, who will prepare your way; the voice of one crying out in the
wilderness: "Prepare the way of the Lord, make his paths straight". John the
baptizer appeared in the wilderness ...

       Mark 1.1–4a NRSV

into the cave

Where do you go when you need to push the limits of your
understanding, capability or experience? The men and women

who became perhaps the earliest recognizable Christian monastics made their way into the deserts of Judea, Sinai and Egypt from the second century CE onwards. Many were driven by the desire to follow the example of Jesus himself, who discovered the desert to be the place of testing, encounter and ultimately affirmation. The much retold account of his 40-day temptation in the wilderness had become a foundational story for these people, one that seemed to point the way to a closer union with him. The desert was the place where the Christ's calling and readiness was sharpened and confirmed. So it would become the place where their own sense of purpose and fitness for the task would be honed and proved.

These earliest religious were also embracing the spirit of John the Baptizer, an apparently wild character who according to all the Gospel writers appeared in the Judaean wilderness, signalling the great coming near of the life of God with his apocalyptic images and water rituals. What setting could be more appropriate for his world-changing message than the desert – stark and testing, beautiful but beyond control. And so this would be the place for the first monastics to express their own radical devotion to God's coming near in the person of Jesus.

These earliest religious were also following an even older way, entering into the imagination and the footsteps of some of the ancient prophets of Judah-Israel. These were the change-proclaimers of the wilderness and the desert place; like the prophet Elijah who fled to the wilderness and lay down under a tree to die; like the prophet Ezekiel who stumbled into a death-valley littered with bones, conjuring up in him an image that still provokes and disturbs today; and like the prophet Isaiah who came to imagine the stark and arid desert as being the very place where one great day the colourful and fecund life of God would break out, unrestrained:

> The wilderness and the dry land shall be glad,
> the desert shall rejoice and blossom;
> like the crocus it shall blossom abundantly,

and rejoice with joy and singing ...
For waters shall break forth in the wilderness,
and streams in the desert;
the burning sand shall become a pool,
and the thirsty ground springs of water;
the haunt of jackals shall become a swamp,
the grass shall become reeds and rushes.

Isaiah 35.1–2a, 6b–7 NRSV

Some of the earliest monastics were also motivated by that compelling but disturbing religious impulse towards self-sacrifice. When the early martyrdom of Christians in the Roman empire gave way, under the emperor Constantine in the early fourth century, to toleration and even advancement for practitioners of their religion, a new generation of Christ-followers sought to find an alternative kind of martyrdom in the testing and belonging of the desert.

Inspired by the desert experience of Jesus, by the desert location of John the Baptizer, by the desert proclaiming prophets, and in some cases by the idea of finding a new and costly martyrdom, a move to the wilderness began. Initially this seems to have been a spontaneous and haphazard flow of individuals setting themselves up in caves and shelters, disconnected from others, an *eremitic* or *hermit* movement (the word *eremitic* has Greek roots meaning something like '*desert*' and '*uninhabited*'). But in time this pattern evolved as many of these proto-monks and nuns began to discover the advantages of sharing their spiky pieces of desert with a few others. The toughness of wilderness living, the discovery of the importance of shared practice, and the necessity for shared wisdom (the writings of the Desert Fathers and Mothers are full of references to wise fathers and mothers) led to the creation of the first Christian monastic settlements – small *sketes* of humble dwellings gathered together, where each monk had their own shelter, but with some shared communal space.

The earliest religious had thus discovered that absolute or permanent solitude is not for most of us, and that some degree of community is good and even necessary. They discovered that the repetition of prayer and the practice of action somehow work best in the company of others – and are more easily honed in a place of simplicity. In time these discoveries would assist the evolution of religious life further into *cenobitic* monasticism (*cenobitic* is derived from Greek words for 'common' and 'life'), with community life forming in the context of a permanent shared monastic settlement – the emphasis I am describing in this book as 'refectory'.

However, whether entered into in the company of others or in solitude, the practice of stillness, study and prayer – what I am referring to as the cave – had become firmly established as a central feature of the religious life, shaping every monastic movement since. So what might cave-dwelling look like in 'regular life'?

mouth to the dust

A health warning may be necessary at this point. Cave-dwelling is a demanding enterprise, and there is, perhaps not surprisingly, a hint of madness that runs through the experience of the early desert monastics. The search for whatever is truly valuable is rarely easy – a discovery that rings true throughout the millennia of human experience. The earliest monks sensed that any authentic seeking after God would require everything of them. If the Holy was to be encountered, that encounter would surely take place away from the distraction of all the busyness and the comfort of human society – among the stones, under the sun, in the cave.

They learned (famously), as articulated by Desert Father Abba Moses, that 'your cell will teach you everything' (Ward, p. 139). The journey to knowing God must include the discipline of coming to know yourself, and that risky journey invariably starts in silence. Solitude, the monastics learned, is vital. There are no shortcuts. In aloneness everything that we imagine is us (but is not really us) falls away. We come to see that much of what we surround ourselves with is just a facade. We begin to know ourselves. This will almost certainly be uncomfortable, at least at first.

These proto-monks discovered, as had their mentor Jesus, that when we go into solitude the 'wild beasts' will make their appearance (Mark 1. 13). Try being in silence or solitude and you will soon make this discovery for yourself. Contrary perhaps to some perceptions, a retreat can sometimes turn out to be less some gentle downtime, more of a journey into a dark wild wood, with wolves circling. But if this experience is uncomfortable, in time it may bring freedom. These first monastics learned through their experience of aloneness, deprivation and darkness that it is possible to confront our fears; that the opposite of – and antidote to – fear is love; and that we are at the very centre of a relentless Love that carries all before it.

The idea of the cave in the monastic tradition teaches us that there will be seasons of life, moments in our routine, times of the day, when we need to strip from ourselves all that clutters, comforts and soothes us. We need to go down to the bare rock floor, alone and vulnerable, face in the dirt, to experience what the ancient Jewish writer of the book of Lamentations experienced:

> to sit alone in silence
> when the Lord has imposed it,
> to put one's mouth to the dust
> (there may yet be hope)
>   Lamentations 3.28–29 NRSV

Where do you go when the tidal wave of stuff coming your way threatens to break on you and consume you? Where do you go when the mad accumulation of debris in your head begins to block all entry and exit points? Where do you go when you need to discover that you are loved, and to hear again – as the great medieval English contemplative Mother Julian of Norwich reminds us – that 'all will be well'? Where do you go when you need to explore the possibility of God-who-is-good? The floor of the cave, mouth to the dust, may surprisingly be the place where we discover what we need.

finding caves, creating encounter spaces

Interest in the rather enigmatic concept of 'spirituality', in Mystery and even prayer is greater than it has been for a long while. From the illusions of Derren Brown to the books of Dan Brown there's something interesting going on here that is worthy of our attention. The cave experience in the monastic tradition highlights the dynamic possibility of encounter with whatever or whoever is beyond our current understanding – the Holy, the Divine, the Mystery, god. Countless lives devoted to prayer mean that the monastics have so much to teach us about clearing the way for encounter. There is great wisdom and learning in their patient rhythm of prayer through day and night, their praying of the Psalms, their rootedness in scripture and their attention to the great garden of creation. There is also much to learn in their deliberate cultivation of space for silence, their ease with stillness and their pattern of withdrawal and engagement.

My observation is that many emerging Christ-following communities are relatively good at action, but perhaps less at ease with pursuing stillness. Both are vital, and the more action-orientated we are, perhaps the more we need a focus on being still. So the finding of caves – the creation of potential encounter spaces – may be a key contribution that new communities shaped around the Jesus tradition can make to the enabling of a better world.

What might happen if a community comes to see itself as having a primary calling to create such spaces? If potential encounter with the Mystery, with the Holy, with God is imagined to be possible, then attention switches from us, and from what *we* do and what *we* offer, to the other. Safe Space, a community in Telford in the UK who are influenced by the monastic tradition, exemplify this emphasis and are 'attempting to create safe spaces to be met by god, embraced, held and loved by god'.[1]

There need to be imaginative attempts to do this. The way most of us live means that we don't have the ability to meet regularly throughout the week. For many people it is impossible to meet in the same place at the same time each day. So various communities are offering online resources. The Morning Bell[2] call to prayer that goes out each day by text, email and twitter is an attempt to offer an encounter space, and a way into a monastic rhythm of prayer. The fact that a large number of other people are sharing the call to pray at the same time, and praying with the prayer, somehow creates a shared sense of encounter.

the cave: a practice

In the Orthodox Christian tradition it has long been practice to create an icon corner as a focus for prayer in the home. In the spirit of this practice I have found it really helpful to create a simple prayer space – a kind of monastic cave – in our home. This can also be done in the garden or even perhaps, with the appropriate permissions, in the workplace. Possible ingredients – depending on one's tradition or inclination – might include an icon, a candle, a praying figure and a copy each of the Psalms and Gospels. The Orthodox icon corner is often full of icons, carrying a sense that the pray-er is accompanied, even surrounded by the saints and the family of God. Some may prefer a minimalist approach, with a single icon. You might like to mark out the floor area with stones or a cord circle. A cushion, prayer mat or prayer stool takes us closer to the cave floor, and further marks this space as being for a different purpose.

We cannot summon up the spirit of God. We cannot create a holy moment. We cannot manipulate the Divine. What we can do is enter a cave, and help to clear a space for the possibility of encounter. In the Jesus tradition every place is a potential encounter place, every space a sacred space. But the monastic way teaches us that some places are particular gifts, retaining and sharing their sense of being prayed-in and encounter-full. In the same way that our ongoing love for our partner or spouse finds particular expression in the intimacy of our kiss or love-making, the cave or prayer space can be the setting in which our wider awareness of and love for the Holy can reveal itself. Like the kiss, like the making of love, this encounter space both emerges from and calls us into a whole life of love and affection, attention and devotion to the loved one.

The journey to the cave is a tough one, but it must not be avoided. And in time, with openness and dedication, we may discover that the dark cave is actually filled with light.

A path from the cave leads to the refectory.

Notes

1 Safespace website: www.safespace.me.uk
2 Morning Bell webpage via: www.ianadams.info
Morning Bell twitter: www.twitter.com/morningbell2u

4

in the refectory – monastic practices of hospitality and commitment to locality, creating communities making an earthy difference for good

What about
the return of the lighthouse keepers?
Keeping lighthouses
not just warning light but
presence
at the cold ocean's edge
with intuition
hope
humanity
being there.
  Ian Adams 'The Lighthouse Keepers'

being there

In time the monastic settlements of the remote desert paved the way for new religious communities located nearer to where most people lived. This was a rediscovery of an ancient Jewish way of life, given renewed emphasis by Jesus of Nazareth – love of God and love of neighbour.

I was on retreat at a priory of Carmelite friars. There was only one other guest – a man in clothing happily mixed rather than carefully matched, with what appeared to be his life possessions crammed into a battered old car. A contemporary gentleman of the road. We sat in the refectory together and he told me that this was how he would be spending the next few months, travelling from priory to monastery to religious house, in the hope and expectation that, at least for while, a warm welcome and generous hospitality would be waiting for him at each place. This had been his experience so far, and he had no doubt that it would be what awaited him.

I like to remember this episode. He was not claiming to be on a worthy retreat to deepen his life of prayer and devotion (which was something like the story I was telling about myself to myself). He was a traveller who needed care – food, shelter and the welcome of fellow human beings. That's not to suggest that religious communities should accept flagrant misuse of their hospitality – most religious communities have worked out ways to avoid this – but that there is something important about simply *being there* for the people who need care, no questions asked, no means assessed, open-handed.

That encounter took place in the refectory, and for this book I'm suggesting the refectory as a symbol of the way of life that an individual or a community seeking to be in the way of the hospitable Jesus might follow. This is the community deciding to offer itself as a source of stability, presence and hospitality to its wider communities. This is the individual seeing their own resources as being a table set for more than one.

'The abbot's table', says St Benedict, 'must always be with guests and travellers' (*The Rule of St Benedict*, ch. 56, Fry p. 77).

One of the dangers in discussing the idea of spirituality is that the conversation – and its practice – can easily become intro-spective. Our spirituality needs to become earthy practice that engages with the scruffy and wonderful world of which we are part. As taught by Jesus, God is loved as (much as) neighbour is loved, and neighbour is loved as (much as) God is loved. There's a wonderful Jewish saying, the spirit of which, if not the current wording, Jesus would have understood: '*Tikkun Olam*', meaning 'repairing the world'. It refers to the actions to which we are called by God in order to help make the world all it can and should

24

be. There is good reason in contemporary Jewish tradition for this emphasis – the ancient prophets of the faith made the same discovery long ago. We have these words from the prophet Micah, who was active in late eighth century BCE in the kingdom of Judah:

> what does the LORD require of you
> but to do justice, and to love Kindness, and to walk humbly
> with your God?   Micah 6.8 NRSV

More than seven centuries later the prophet Micah's theme is taken up by the rabbi Jesus of Nazareth, both in word and action. Perhaps the core of Jesus' teaching is represented by the creedal manifesto known as the Beatitudes in chapter five of Matthew's Gospel, and here we find a powerful flow between personal devotion to God and selfless service to the world:

> Blessed are those who hunger and thirst for righteousness,
>   for they will be filled.
> Blessed are the merciful, for they will receive mercy.
> Blessed are the pure in heart, for they will see God.
>   Matthew 5.6–8 NRSV

The monastic tradition almost always sees itself as being expressed in this flow between prayerful engagement with God and activity on behalf of the world – and specifically on behalf of the most needy. This motion invariably begins simply as presence, being alongside and with those who suffer, sharing their situation and then working to bring relief. This we might call the practice of refectory, beginning with presence, then taking shape in many different ways: caring for the poor, assisting the needy, standing up for the powerless and feeding the hungry. Engagement with and on behalf of those at the bottom of the pile takes us, in the company of the monastics, into deep contact with the Jesus of the Gospels.

Almost all religious orders see the provision of hospitality as a core characteristic and key way to serve the world. So what might a new community look like with a central commitment to hospitality in the name of Jesus, rather than a vague nod in the direction of welcome?

communities of hospitality

Monastic experience shows that hospitality needs to be both intentional and genuine. Many monastic communities, contrary to our perception perhaps, have situated themselves where people are most likely to be. Iona is an interesting example. Like many other pilgrims and visitors, I'm transfixed by its startling beauty and compelling presence. When I go there, as I do once a year, most years, I fetch up on its shore like some sea-battered pebble. I go first up the narrow tarmac road to the north end of the island, then cross the *machair* to the beach. In the spring and summer the air here seems full of wild flower, sand and salt. I find a place to sit, to draw breath, to drink in the setting. Then I walk back to the Abbey. I look for the vague outlines of the cat and the monkey carved into the stone walls of the chancel – a reminder from the Benedictine builders of the abbey of the call to step into that powerful flow between prayer and activity, stillness and action. I move into the south transept, adding my prayers to those of countless monks, islanders, pilgrims and tourists who have been here before. The healing has begun. The hospitality of this place reshapes me.

The long journey to Iona is for me a pilgrimage to a faraway and remote destination. But when the first monastic settlement was founded on the island in the sixth century by Columba and his monks, Iona was not remote to those who lived in that part of the world but a well-visited place. While not having a natural harbour, the relative calm of the sound of Iona means that travellers and their boats are sheltered from the worst of the ocean's storms. The island is a natural stopping point on the west coast of what we now call Scotland. Take a map of north-western Europe and tilt it on its side. Get over the strange sense of disorientation, and the sea suddenly becomes the obvious way to get from A to B, from Ireland to Greenland via the Hebrides. This monastic community on Iona is seen to be not so much at the edge of the world, but on an ancient transport and communication highway.

We are currently seeing a new interest in communities of hospitality, situated where people are and engaging with people in the ways that people now communicate. Some are experimenting with community houses, new kinds of small monastic settlements in the city, such as House 244 in Oxford, the Simple Way in Philadelphia and COTA in Seattle. This can be a wonderful but tough experience – living with people in community soon brings up issues. Community can seem simple and attractive enough as long as it remains an idea. The challenge is actually doing it with others. But the learning from the monastics is that through this process of community-making we can be shaped to be more Christ-like, and the gracious Christ is made known. Other communities are experimenting with online presence – the Anglican cathedral of Second Life[1] and i-Church[2] are examples of this imaginative approach to hospitality, taking seriously the rapid changes that are occurring in the way that we humans relate to each other.

communities of reconciliation

Inspired by Jesus' teaching, 'Blessed are the peacemakers, for they will be called children of God' (Matthew 5.9 NRSV), some monastic communities have found a particular calling to become agents of peace and reconciliation. This impulse played an important role in the ecumenical and multinational nature of the Taizé community in France which began to take shape during the Second World War. The St Egidio Community based in Rome sees peacemaking as a key part of its work: 'Sant'Egidio is a "house of peace" where many have sought and seek the end of conflicts that stain the world with blood.'[3]

The need for reconciliation is ever present at every level of society. And reconciliation rarely happens by itself. Someone has to take the first step, to make the first gesture, and the religious have a particular calling to become that first agent of change. A religious community that is itself a story of reconciliation has a quiet power to effect such change. We can't help others into peace and reconciliation if we are not yet peaceful or reconciled ourselves – but in so far as we take steps in this direction then the possibilities of peace and reconciliation may ripple out, at first a trickle, then a stream, and perhaps a wave of joy and hope. Again this needs to be intentional. The mayBe community in Oxford uses the word *grace* to describe the spirit that it desires and needs to live its life as a reconciling community:

> The journey is a shared journey, and we long for it to be a grace-filled one. And so in mayBe community we have committed ourselves to being peaceful in our exchanges with each other, giving no space to sarcasm or aggression. We are cultivating generosity. We are looking for the good in each other and in ourselves. We are practising forgiveness. We honour each other. We seek to hold each other and each other's fragments that God might bring us back to wholeness.[4]

As in hospitality so in reconciliation, the practice of presence again plays a vital role. Imagine a community of reconciliation inspired by the teaching, example and presence of Jesus-the-peacemaker being present in each neighbourhood, settlement and village. Wonder how life might become very different, truly blessed, as a result for all those who live in anxiety, division, fear or mistrust.

communities of energy

One development in monastic settlement that we see coming into being in Dark Age or Celtic Britain is that of the religious community as a hub for the life of the wider community in which it is set or which grows around it. This kind of monastery became the centre of energy for the local population – source of learning, health care, education and welfare. Some evidence for this has been found in archaeological work at monastic settlement sites. Originally founded in the fifth century by St Machaoi, the settlement at Nendrum on Mahee Island in Strangford Lough, Northern Ireland, is a particularly interesting example of an early Christian Irish monastery because of the early use of stone on this site. The monastic settlement is on an island, suggesting perhaps a desire for solitude but possibly also, as with Iona, a willingness to be accessible via the water, the highway of the time.

Excavations on the site have revealed that the monastery site consisted of three round dry-stone-walled and broadly circular enclosures, one within the other. The innermost enclosure has a church ruin with sundial, the remains of a round tower and a graveyard. The middle enclosure contains remains of huts and workshops. There's evidence of industrial work being carried on in the outer circle. Recent work on the shore has discovered a pier and a tidal mill.

Members of the Telford-based Safe Space community recently visited the site and found the physical layout to be helpful in their attempts to work out how to live in the spirit of the monastics in their setting. For them the Celtic monastic community at Nendrum offered a 'resource-full' model, demonstrating a balance of both solitude and exposure, of being set apart from the wider community and a hub of life for that community. There's a clear understanding in this emphasis that the religious life is not just about prayer and worship – as important as they are – but to do with bringing earthy, local change for good. It's important to recognize that we can't be the solution to every need, but equally important to see that the religious life can be of great good wherever we are. What this will look like will differ, of course, according to setting. So it's worth asking what the needs of the wider community are, and wondering if the religious community might become a source of energy focused on these needs.

the refectory: a practice

The practice of refectory is best done simply. There is something both humble and full of possibility in the simple practice of sharing food with others. The mayBe community in Oxford has a weekly community meal as the pivot point of its life. The table becomes the place of hospitality, engagement and encounter. mayBe has learned some valuable lessons on the way: keep the meal simple, for this way everyone can feel that they can host or help to provide the food at some point. Do the preparation and the clearing up together. Give time to all of this. The meal should not be rushed or seen as a means to another end. The sharing of food and the hearing of each other's stories is the making of community. When simple ways are found to let the stories of Jesus enter this mix – and space to wonder what they may mean – interesting things seem to happen. When hospitality, peace and reconciliation are beginning to be lived in this way, they will naturally spill out from us.

And so there is progression and flow in the monastic way: from the cave – place of grounding, self-recovery, God discovery; to the refectory – place of hospitality, reconciliation and energy for our wider communities.

And then out on to the road, place of surprising encounter.

Notes

1 Anglican Cathedral of Second Life website: slangcath.wordpress.com

2 i-Church website: www.i-church.org

3 'From the poor to peace', document on the website of St Egidio: www. santegidio.org

4 'the spirit of mayBe' on the mayBe website: www.maybe.org.uk

5

on the road – the experience of friars inspiring creative engagement in the wider world

I know the fragrant theory
that to welcome strangers
is to entertain angels
but the reality
is
more pungent

> Ian Adams 'Fragrant theory (man in a stained sheepskin coat on
>   Magdalen Bridge)'

The stooping figure of my mother, waist deep in the grass and caught there like a piece of sheep's wool, was the last I saw of my country home as I left it to discover the world ... It was 1934. I was nineteen years old, still soft at the edges, but with a confident belief in good fortune. I carried a small rolled-up tent, a violin in a blanket, a change of clothes, a tin of treacle biscuits, and some cheese. I was excited, vain-glorious, knowing I had far to go; but not as yet, how far.

> Laurie Lee, *As I Walked Out One Midsummer Morning*

on the road

For the first time in my life I find myself living near the sea. Most times that I go to the beach I enact a small ritual which I've been doing for years. It won't change the world, but it is what it is. I go down to the water's edge and, attempting to avoid a drenching, try to cup some water to splash on my face. I sing a line from an old song – heh it's me! – then set myself down to look out west on to the sea. I'm pretty easy to please, so this always makes me feel better.

There's something romantic about life on the open road, the flowing river or the boundless ocean. The unfolding is full of possibility, and poets, musicians and writers find it to be an endless source of inspiration. But the same road that carries some to adventure brings hints of trouble to others. The default position for many local communities with regard to travellers coming their way is a mix of suspicion, intrigue and fear. The authorities often find it hard to cope, in any sense, with travelling communities. What is it that makes us nervous about travellers? Perhaps their travelling life asks an implicit question of the majority of us who are in one place. Why are you where you are?

There's a repeating pattern in the development of the religious life down the centuries relating to the open road, the flowing river and the boundless ocean. At key points it seems that some monastics always sense a call to leave the demanding security of the enclosure to face the demanding insecurity of the open road. Neither is better than the other. Both are good and true. Both are necessary. They express different aspects of human life lived to the full.

Perhaps we need to go somewhere to discover that *here* is as good as *any*where. Perhaps we need to keep moving until we absorb the wisdom that a new setting will not provide the answer to our own dilemmas, for we take ourselves with us, and we need to come home to ourselves. And perhaps we need to go some-where to keep on remembering what it's like not to belong, and to be in solidarity with those who are not yet able to find a home.

The religious life has a particular contribution to make in this story of movement and encounter. It may be grounded in silence and seclusion, but it is made real in the everyday life of people wherever they are. A theological term for this process is incarna-tion. The God that emerges in the Judaeo-Christian stream is experienced not only in our quiet interior, but in the mess, the wonder and the mundanity of everyday living. This was the radical and even shocking idea that was working away in John, the aged disciple of Jesus, for many years after the Christ's death and resurrection, eventually welling up in him to produce the stunning opening to his Gospel:

> And the Word became flesh and lived among us, and we have seen his glory, the glory as of a father's only son, full of grace and truth.　　　　　　　　　　　　　　　　　John 1.14 NRSV

Reflecting on the life of Jesus, John's conclusion is that God had somehow taken human form in this man; that amazingly, Jesus was somehow the life of God uttered (the Word) into the world, resounding across time, recognized by some with 'ears to hear', but ringing with hope for all. As Jesus was encountered, and missed or recognized then, so he may be encountered, and missed or recognized now, in the faces of the people we meet and even in ourselves, carriers of the signs of Christ's presence. So look again at the crazy guy on the street, listen to the young student in the class, talk with the elderly woman at the bus stop, hear the excited kids at the playground. Christ may not be far from here.

There is great value in stability, but the spiritual search has a dynamic quality. A significant stream of monastic life always begins to flow from the deep pools of the religious enclosure. The stream flows where it will, unafraid to encounter whoever and whatever it finds. This is the way of the friar.

travel light into exile

The various orders of travelling friars found inspiration for their life of movement in the Gospels. Jesus seems to have a spent a lot of time on the road, saying famously that 'foxes have holes, and birds of the air have nests; but the Son of Man has nowhere to lay his head' (Matthew 8.20). On many occasions in the Gospels this first century rabbi is recorded as bringing life-changing encounter to the people he meets as he walks. In Matthew's Gospel we find a foundational saying of Jesus for all types and orders of friar:

> As you go, proclaim the good news, 'The kingdom of heaven has come near.' Cure the sick, raise the dead, cleanse the lepers, cast out demons. You received without payment; give without payment. Take no gold, or silver, or copper in your belts, no bag for your journey, or two tunics, or sandals, or a staff; for labourers deserve their food. Whatever town or village you enter, find out who in it is worthy, and stay there until you leave.
>
> Matthew 10.7–11 NRSV

Jesus calls his followers to go and share the good news of God's life come near. This is to be proclaimed in words – a calling accepted with relish by the Dominican friars, who saw preaching on the road as a primary calling. But the good news is also to be given shape through action, in curing the sick, through bringing the outcast leper back cleansed into community, through casting out evil spirits, and even astonishingly by raising of the dead. Inspired by this kind of teaching, St Francis famously kissed a leper and in so doing created a pattern of behaviour on the road for the friars who adopted his way of following the Christ.

Jesus' instructions go further. The disciple-friar is to take no means of payment, and the minimum of clothing and footwear. This is demanding teaching, and we should be amazed at the courage and tenacity of the friar communities who have taken its demands seriously. But take it seriously they have – and in the context of the religious life we see a constant flow from cave to refectory to road, a persistent impulse to move from wilderness to settlement to highway.

The early monastics in the desert also embraced something that had been faced more than once before by the people of Jesus' ancient faith tradition – the experience of exile. For the Jewish people this dislocation and removal from all that they knew and loved had been a regular possibility and reality throughout their history. The early monastics saw their own experience of desert exile as an identification with a wider human experience of dislocation. We can see this tradition being carried on in the experience of the peregrini, the travelling monks of western Europe in the so called Dark or Celtic age. Their journeying is representative of a wider human experience of exile. And their commitment to journeying without the security of destination is a sign of hope. The exile will come to an end, a home will be found again.

For peregrini like Brendan the Navigator, the sixth-century Irish monastic who set sail out into the Atlantic Ocean, the exile of journey without the security of safe transport or guaranteed destination was a declaration that God was good and could be trusted. And so it may be that in our times individuals and communities who learn in some way to take the road, the path of exile, may be able to offer hope to all who feel exiled, lost or without hope.

the travelling band

In the Gospels, Jesus is often pictured on the road with his followers. Some of his most interesting encounters happen here, with the sort of person he may not otherwise have met in a society riddled with a large measure of patriarchy, xenophobia and fear. So Jesus meets women, strangers, occupying soldiers, the diseased and the outcast. There's a memorable scene in Martin Scorsese's often brilliant film, *The Last Temptation of Christ*, in which the Jesus character sets out for Jerusalem. At first he's seen walking through the wilderness with five disciples – Judas, James, John, Andrew and Simon – then gradually more figures join the group, until it's a large travelling band. It's a simple but powerful picture of a community on the move with fluidity, dynamism and purpose.

It seems to me that the travelling band of friar-disciples has much to offer us as a picture of religious community taking seriously its call to both seek after God and to be engaged with the wider world. It carries the good news to where people are and lives it there alongside people. It creates space for all kinds of people to experience something of the life of the community. Some will join the travelling band for a while and then leave to take another path (sometimes a parallel one). Others will elect to make their accompanying and their being accompanied more permanent. And that image of accompanying is a powerful one in this context. When the whole community sees itself as a travelling band, it becomes clear that all are learning, all are aspiring-to-become. No one has 'arrived'; all are on the journey.

the road as teacher

It's interesting how often in the Gospels the better-world-now for which we all yearn (the one that Jesus spoke of as 'the Kingdom of God come near') often takes shape in the uncontrollable environment that is the open space, the street or the market place. The road is full of surprise and a place, if we are open to it, of learning. Francis made a life-changing discovery on the street. Even Jesus seems to have learned things on the road. There's an intriguing incident recorded in the Gospel of Mark (7.24–29) where Jesus meets a woman who asks for him to 'cast out a demon' from her daughter. Jesus' initial response to this woman – a foreigner – is abrupt and dismissive. The woman, however, is strong and witty and she persists in her request. Jesus hears her response and changes direction. The act of exorcism is given, the blessing offered.

The friar understands that the open space requires us to surrender our control. We are vulnerable on the road. 'Have a safe journey', we say. 'Call us when you get there', urge anxious parents. Travel can be an anxious business. Home is so much safer. But there is something vital about this human experience of stepping out into the unknown with little but our equivalent of Laurie Lee's 'small rolled-up tent, a violin in a blanket, a change of clothes, a tin of treacle biscuits, and some cheese'. The encounters that come our way will bring valuable learning. We will learn more about life, about love, about fear and about people.

The experience of friar-disciples is that on the road we may also learn something about the companionship of the God-man Jesus, our fellow traveller; something about the guiding of the God-Spirit, full of surprise; and something about the constancy of the God-Parent, drawing us on. Learning on the road can happen in all directions to those who are open to it. The disciple learns from the person encountered, the person encountered learns from the disciple.

storytelling in the open

One of the well-documented themes of an emerging Christianity in the last few years has been the consistent attempt to be in so-called 'secular space'. Of course in this experimentation the rediscovery is made again and again that there is no such thing as secular space. Every place is holy, every place can be encounter space with the Divine. And when groups or communities take the journey into the secular space of park, cafe or pub they become much more accessible. The contemporary travelling band seems to attract and collect people on the way. Strangers, friends and friends of friends join the lived story as it happens.

There is great energy and possibility in public storytelling. The mayBe community in Oxford began to gather outdoors because we had nowhere else to go, and because we simply liked it. Gradually it became part of the life and the story of the community. The ancient riverside field known as Portmeadow became, we said, 'like a cathedral to us', and the drama of the eucharist seemed to overcome our lack of holy table and vestments easily enough, simply asking to be received, shared and enjoyed. The parables and sayings of Jesus took on a new vitality as we looked for lost things, considered the lilies, allowed the weeds and flowers to grow around us, and watched the sky.

The friars, of course, knew this all along. They have been telling the stories of hope in the open for centuries, with humour, imagination, and even scandal – Francis famously made a particular point by stripping naked in the street. Art in the market place, story telling in public space and ritual released into the open, I suggest, are creative contemporary takes on the ancient way of the friars, and are full of possibility as we look for ways to live the story of hope in tough times.

the road: a practice

So how might we take something of this friar aspect of the religious life into our everyday life? I recommend walking. If you can, wherever you live and work, start to walk. And be open to the possibility of encounter. This will sometimes feel like a gift, at other times it will be demanding. On the road we meet whatever and whoever comes our way.

In Jesus' instructions to his soon-to-be travelling disciples he encouraged them to bring a sign of peace with them. Each house where they stayed (and, we might imagine, each person they met) was to be offered a blessing of peace (Matthew 10.12–13). You'll have to work out what your greeting might be – I suggest that it needs to fit who you are and your setting. It may also reflect in some way, in word or spirit, the house greeting of Jesus, so something like 'peace to this house' or the greeting of the risen Jesus according to the Gospels of Luke and John, 'peace be with you' (Luke 24.36 and John 20.19, 21, 26). Whatever the wording, what truly matters is the authenticity of the greeting, whatever the words or signs you use. Receive Christ's peace, carry it with you, share it.

So far this exploration into the possibility of taking monastic spirituality into contemporary living has concentrated on the flow from place to place, the setting of personal and community life – what I am calling cave, refectory and road. The focus changes now to wonder how the rhythms and emphases of monastic life, wherever it is lived, might shape a new earthy spirituality wherever we are.

Time to imagine some new rhythms.

6

rhythm of life – the traditional monastic rule of life reinterpreted, bringing freedom and creativity through a new understanding of time

Each time
I return to the island
I am lifted
I resolve
to live in the spirit of the Columcille
who was shaped here
rock hard edge
swept, scoured, sculpted,
into warm stone reflecting light

Ian Adams, 'The island'

A person who wishes to begin a good life should be like a man who draws a circle. Let him get the center in the right place and keep it so and the circumference will be good. In other words, let a man first learn to fix his heart on God and then his good deeds will have virtue; but if a man's heart is unsteady, even the great things he does will be of small advantage.

Meister Eckhart, *From Whom God Hid Nothing*[1]

Put your hands to work, and your hearts to God.
Mother Ann Lee, founder of the Shakers, 1736–84

meister eckhart's circle

I draw a circle in the sand. I step into the centre and sit. Giving attention to my breathing, I begin to breathe more slowly, more deeply. I let a short prayer take shape, and repeat it in silence as I breathe in and out. But now my anxieties are making themselves known, a drone of hyperactivity. I become aware of the tension in my shoulders. Again I breathe slowly, more deeply. I let the prayer word form. The pattern repeats itself:

> A stance of stillness.
> Breathe deep and slow.
> Let a prayer word form.
> Anxiety surfaces.
> Tension.
> Focus again on breathing.
> Return to the prayer word.
> Back into stillness.
> Slowly, eventually, a subtle change, a calm of sorts.
> Keep on.

Contemporary life, for most of us, is lived at a fast pace. And Christianity has not always offered its best learning and practice to those of us in thrall to speed. For too long, in too many places, Christianity has been portrayed or perceived as being primarily a belief system. The Church has sometimes colluded with this distortion of the way of the teacher Jesus. 'I believe', 'we believe' have been our default positions. Christianity is not alone in this. Other religions have tended to slide in the same direction, sometimes with catastrophic results. Of course, belief matters. Belief affects what we do and how we behave. It gives us a vital grounding and offers us a crucial source of stability. But reliance on belief alone can also leave us indifferent, arrogant and isolated from the realities of human existence.

Inspired by the teacher Jesus, and by the monastics who practised his way, I want to imagine an alternative to religion as purely belief system. I want to suggest religion as a discovery of balance; religion as a mix of being and doing; religion as prayer and practice; as self-awareness and self-giving. Taking a lead from the Dominican teacher Meister Eckhart, I suggest that religion can be 'the drawing of a circle', a 'fixing of the heart', and spinning out from that centre a life of devotion to people, to planet and to God.

There's a beach near to our home in South Devon where I work with people on retreat to improvise a response to Eckhart's picture. Using driftwood or stones we each draw a big circle in the sand. The circle is full of light. It's provisional (the tide will sweep over it soon enough), but it seems to have a simple strength. Some of our circles touch or overlap. When they are all drawn, each person finds their circle-centre, and we place ourselves there. To sit or stand in the centre of the circle, facing the sea, can be a profound experience. A symbolic relocating of ourselves at the fixed point that is God's presence, God's love, God's being. We draw breath and fall silent. We find a prayer, or a prayer finds us. Everything seems to settle into its rightful place.

a different measure

The traditional monastic rule of life is a daily 'drawing of a circle'. The monastic rule of life helps the monk to enter into the flows of minute and hour, of day and night, of dawn and dusk, of day and week, of season and feast day and, ultimately, of life and death. This is life lived to a different measure, with different priorities.

I want to suggest that the monastic rule of life can be re-interpreted and embraced by people in the 'regular world' as a rhythm of life that will enable us to give attention to what truly matters, and to re-imagine human being, starting with us.

There's a frozen food company in the UK, some of whose trucks carry the slogan, 'because life's too short to peel carrots'. But the religious life suggests that not only is there plenty of time to peel carrots, but that the peeling of carrots, when approached in the right way, brings freedom. Strangely, perhaps, for something that looks as if it might bring with it extra pressures – even more stuff to do in even less time – the monastic rhythm of life has the power to release us from the tyranny of time-deficit.

The monastic rule of life sets priorities, and because it knows our preference, if given the chance, for the easy way out (mea culpa), it anticipates our hiding places. But it also raises our sights to what may be possible. This will take – initially at least – a great deal of effort and application. Why do we so often choose to live to inferior rhythms and faltering beats? The great saint Paul knew this aspect of the human predicament well. 'I can will what is right, but I cannot do it' (Romans 7.18b NRSV). Most of us, most of the time, seem to need some help to do the good thing that is within us.

There's currently a renewed and welcome interest in various disciplines in doing things at the right speed. In Philip Groning's 2006 film *Into Great Silence* – a beautiful observation of life in a Carthusian monastery – there's a wonderful scene in which a monk prepares and cuts cloth for a habit for a new brother. There's neither undue haste, nor a wasting of time. But rather, deliberate care, attention and love for the task. The viewer experiences an unfolding sense of wonder that such a quiet undertaking can be so full of meaning.

The monastic rhythm of life cultivates a different approach to time. It redefines the task as not just a means to an end, but as something to do because it is in itself both necessary and good. Its particular and brilliant gift is to carve out space for what is truly important. The monastic day does not, for example, allow the flexibility to stay on at work because of a deadline. The things we are most likely to drop – prayer, silence and stillness – are given particular attention and pride of place in the monastic diary.

On hearing the signal for an hour of the divine office, the monk will immediately set aside what he has in hand and go with utmost speed, yet with gravity and without giving occasion to frivolity. Indeed, nothing is to be preferred to the Work of God (*The Rule of St Benedict*, ch. 43, Fry, p. 65).

When the day and the night are lived this way it becomes

clear that most of our hurrying is unnecessary, and perhaps even harmful. The monastics teach us that waiting may be a key stance in life, in their case waiting to see what, in God's care, is coming into being. A waiting stance will, of course, need cultivating. It will need work. It will require us to adopt a new rhythm.

morning bell: a daily rhythm of life

The monastic day starts early.

At 4.30am each day the men and women of the ecumenical community at Bose in northern Italy are 'invited to wake up and to dedicate at least an hour to personal Lectio Divina (prayerful reading of Scripture) on a passage of the Bible chosen by the community'.[2] So the day begins, and between now and 8pm the day is marked out by a framework for daily life that seeks to give balance and attention to what is truly important. This is the simple, if demanding, genius of the monastic day: the creation of space for what is truly essential.

At Bose there are community prayers at 6am, 12.30pm and 6.30pm. Silence is kept from 7am for an hour, and during lunch. The work of the community is undertaken from 8am until 12 noon, and again from 2pm until 5pm. The evening meal is accompanied by conversation. On Saturday evenings the community gathers for a vigil in preparation for the Sunday Eucharist. At the end of each day, from 8pm, the 'great silence' is entered and kept through what remains of the evening and through the night.

The religious community is much better placed than most of us to resist the temptation to let demands, deadlines or delays reshape our day for worse. The monastery bell is rung, and attention moves to what needs attention. There is, of course, a testing rigour to this daily rhythm. It requires persistence, attention and repetition.

I am trying to learn to play the guitar and the mandolin. There are no shortcuts. Believe me, I've looked for them. My fingers seem to learn the stretches and patterns only through repetition. My arm needs continual practice to access the rhythm. The religious life teaches us the value of repetition. The monk George Guiver CR makes the point about the value of repetition in the area of the daily monastic office (daily prayer) – what he calls stream prayer:

> The effect is that of a stream, slowly wearing away stones and banks ... Stream prayer builds up deposits over a long time. Its under-the-skin working in liturgical prayer is similar to the experience of learning a language in a foreign country. Anyone who has that experience will know how the language builds up inside quite imperceptibly.   Guiver, *Company of Voices*, p. 23

There are, of course, many streams pouring over us and around us, all the time. It may be worth wondering which streams we choose to allow to wear away our rough edges and build up their deposits within us. The monastic rhythm of life is an exposure to the ancient stream of prayer and the possibility of God. It's not a spectacular process, but its mark is deep and lasting.

A key element in the monastic rhythm of life is the praying of the Psalms, which have always been the songbook and the prayer mat of the Jewish and Christian faiths. Monastic communities have long understood that whatever we are feeling, we don't need to reach far into the Psalms before finding that the Psalm writer has been there before us. The Psalm-composers have done it all and seen it all. Despair. Sickness. Loss. Fear. Hate. Addiction. Joy. Hope. Peace. Lifting. Love. The Psalms give us a vocabulary for what we are feeling. They help us to be real with ourselves and with God. The Community of Bose sings the entire Psalter (the biblical collection of Psalms) every two weeks. The Gospels are at the centre of the community's meditation, and the stories and prophecies, hopes and lamentations of the Old Testament combine with them to weave a deep pattern into the background of community life.

making vows: creating a rhythm of life

The religious rhythm of life is invariably given substance and
boundaries by vows. Vow-taking is perhaps for many of us now a
less familiar part of life than it has been in a very long while. But
we still recognize its importance. Promises made, promises kept
and promises broken are the stuff of human society. Vows give
shape to our aspirations. They act as a threshold moment of
change. This is how things will be from this point, this is my
commitment, this is our agreement.

Traditionally the vows of the monastic community are taken
for life, and only entered into after a lengthy period, usually a
few years, in the testing space of the novitiate. This lifetime
commitment seems to be a particularly hard path, bucking the
current trend for shorter-term commitments. It is perhaps one
reason why many of the traditional religious orders report that
they are facing a future with a diminishing number of people
exploring the possibility of the monastic life.

So how might we take the idea of the monastic rule of life into
the everyday world that most of us inhabit? Over time the meaning of words changes. Phrases find and lose weight, they collect
and shed nuances, gather and scatter images. The word 'rule' has
a harshness and rigidity to it in contemporary culture, which is
why the word 'rhythm' may have more positive resonance at this
time.

I want to suggest a few possibilities for creating a rhythm of
life where you are. One is to explore the rules of life of some
traditional communities; then to run that learning through your
own experience and that of your community. It's important that
any rhythm should emerge out of the life of a community, not be
imposed; it should be agreed and accepted, not forced or man-
ipulated. Where are the points of confluence? What are the aspects
of these rules that we find most difficult – and is there something
for us to learn here? A mixing process of ancient tradition and
contemporary experience can produce a way to live that is both

connected to the past and liveable in our current setting. My experience is that sometimes the tradition has the ability to cut through all our complications. For example, in researching for the vows for the mayBe community in Oxford we found the wisdom of the communities of Bose and Taizé really helpful. In seeking to understand what the role of our prior or abbot might look like we found this phrase from Bose really helpful:

> The community seeks to live monastic life in our own time under the guidance of a rule and a spiritual father, the prior, whose duty it is to point the community at all times towards the one true light of the Gospel of Jesus Christ.[2]

As the abbot of the community I found that phrase to be both demanding and enlightening. Everything I was called to do and be needed to sit within that shape. I soon discovered, of course, that the duty to 'point the community at all times towards the one true light of the Gospel of Jesus Christ' started with me, a demanding daily undertaking. If I wasn't orientated in the direction of the Christ it was going to be difficult to suggest to my sisters and brothers that they orientate themselves in that direction.

It may be that there is merit in exploring the idea of taking vows for a season, a cycle or a year. This is perhaps one area (another might be celibacy) where 'real monasticism' and any contemporary take on monasticism set in the wider community among 'regular people' might agree to take different paths. Of course vows for a season, a cycle or year will feel different from lifetime vows, but in an age of potentially constant movement and switching of roles, even short-term vows may have an impact.

So mayBe community makes annual vows each Advent, vows which focus on the spirit of the community and its calling to be a 'community exploring creative, simple, engaged and playful living in the way of Jesus'. Each person in the community is invited to make a vow to follow in the way of Christ in the company of the community, and the abbot and each of the seven guardians of the community make an additional vow to follow their own particular callings within the community. Coupled with the making of these vows is a recognition that the keeping of these vows will not be an easy thing. 'With the help of God and your prayers I will' is the vow-taker's humble response to the questions received, a welcome understanding as the community faces the toughness of the task.

Perhaps the most important thing in this area is to create a simple rhythm of life – and to live it from the start. In a community context this means committing to a way of life even if there are only a handful of you. If 'more' people seems important (and it need not), set out as if there *were* more of you. Both the communities of Bose and Taizé started out very small – with Br Roger at Taizé and Br Enzo at Bose, and in each case just a few friends and supporters. It will become what it will become. Make the community rhythm of life simple, and stick to it. And some learning from mayBe: incorporate a sabbath – the community lives a seven-week cycle, taking a sabbath or sabbatical of a week every seven weeks (or thereabouts depending on public holidays). This gives the community more time to devote to families and friends on a frequent basis, and seems to reinvigorate the community at the start of each new cycle.

rhythm of life: a practice

Here's a simple practice to incorporate into a personal rhythm of life wherever you are. I call this Meister Eckhart's circle.

Make a circle, tracing it in the air around you, or using string or pebbles.
Find the centre of the circle.
Sit or stand there, adopt a stance of stillness.
Focus on your breathing, breathe deep and slow.
Let a prayer word form within you, and add it silently to your breathing.

When anxiety surfaces or tension comes, focus again on your
   breathing.
Keep returning to your prayer word.
Find your way back into stillness.
Slowly, eventually, a subtle change, a calm of sorts.
Commit to this.

Ian Adams, 'The Practice of Meister Eckhart's Circle'

Notes

1 *Meister Eckhart, From Whom God Hid Nothing*, by Meister Eckhart, edited by David O'Neal, ©1996 by David O'Neal. pp. 5–6 Reprinted by arrangement with Shambhala Publications Inc., Boston, MA. www.shambhala.com
   2 The Community of Bose website: www.monasterodibose.it

spiritual formation – monastic learning practices and becoming more (beauti)fully human in the way of Jesus

I thought I was dead;
lost
in the dark damp earth
buried
unknowing

but in the deep
you were forming me
a seed planted
tended
loved
awaited
becoming

    Ian Adams, 'Lost'

There is nothing more important than prayer;
therefore, our greatest attention and most diligent attention must attend it.
    St Theophan the Recluse 1815–94

go to checkout

In the so-called developed world we live at a time when, until recently, pretty much everything has been available, at a price, and if not now, then 'almost now'. Experiences have been procured, products bought, information gathered. It was all there. Ready to go. Just in time. Waiting for you. Go to checkout. But the current worldwide economic crisis has brought uncertainty to the mix and questioned the whole basis on which we have been living. The checkout has begun to look a little different. No longer the site of gratification but the place where we are scrabbling in our pockets for any credit card with some space left on it. The state of the environment and persistent conflicts around the world add extra complexity to the situation.

So what's left? Where is our sense of well-being located? On what can we depend? Oddly enough for a society so high on the immediate, we rarely seemed content to focus on the moment. Instead we were working towards an imagined future, a para-doxical vision characterized by yearning and disgust, a hollow and ambiguous dream of a better way. Now even that future looks bleak.

So how might the monastic stream help us negotiate our strange twenty-first-century experience, where we can find ourselves amazed, uncertain, bored and screwed up, all at the same time? What are we – and what can we become as human beings? It seems to me that the monastic tradition has much to offer in the area of our formation – as followers of the Christ, to be sure, but also in the wider attempt for us to learn how to be human.

into stillness

The religious life begins in stillness. However, this may not only be the simplest of disciplines, it may also be the hardest. With stillness comes vulnerability. We know how awkward it can be to share a room in silence with a stranger. But there's something vital about this discipline. Stillness forces us to confront our reliance on activity. Silence reveals our addiction to noise. Stillness and silence serve to examine our attachments. Both bring into the light our sense of who we are. They help us come home to ourselves.

The monastic experience is that when we become still, and when we enter into silence, we may actually discover there a sense of belonging, hope and even love. In stillness the monk's fears and uncertainties begin to recede as our existence is discovered to have a core of benevolence running through it. This doesn't mean that bad, even terrible things don't happen, but the monastics report an experience of essential goodness that cannot be overwhelmed. 'I no longer fear God, but I love him', said the Desert Father Abba Anthony, 'for love casts out fear' (Ward, p. 8). If the risks of entering into silence are high, the rewards are even greater. Mother Julian, 1342–1423 Christian mystic and anchoress (living a hermit-type life enclosed in a small cell attached to St Julian's church in Norwich) had a series of visions of Jesus which she recorded as 'showings':

> There is no created being who can know how much and how sweetly and how tenderly the Creator loves us. And therefore we can with his grace and his help persevere in spiritual contemplation, with endless wonder at this high, surpassing, immeasurable love which our Lord in his goodness has for us.
>
> Edmund Colledge and James Walsh,
> *Julian of Norwich: Showings*, p. 186

People who have devoted themselves to prayer down the millennia are usually very clear about the importance of the self-observance that comes in the practice of stillness. Know yourself. Become self-aware. This is the message of Evagrius, another fourth-century Desert Father who lived in the Egyptian desert, as well as having periods of city-dwelling in Constantinople, Jerusalem and Alexandria. In his instructions to monks he writes this:

Sit in your cell, collecting your thoughts. Remember the day of your death. See then what the death of your body will be; let your spirit be heavy, take pains, condemn the vanity of the world, so as to be able to live always in the peace you have in view without weakening.

Ward, p. 63

Each of us has to deal with life as it comes, and we each have our patterns of thought and behaviour to help us cope. For monks like Evagrius, these patterns are not the real us, but are rather the various ways that we have developed to enable us to handle whatever comes in our direction. To realize this is to learn to sit outside of ourselves and begin to see what is going in our often frantic minds, a process that the Augustinian friar Martin Laird OSA describes as going 'from victim to witness' (Laird, *Into the Silent Land*, p. 95). This quest requires us to be real – to see through our devices, our defences and our manipulations – even through our good points, so that we see ourselves as we really are: part of teeming humanity and yet each of us gloriously unique, capable of giving and denying love, yet always beloved, capable at times of stooping pretty low, and yet also having the ability to reach the heights. The formational possibilities of stillness and silence, as lived and taught by the religious down the centuries, are great.

Devote yourself to the art of discerning the divine presence and become a witness to this presence (Rule of Bose 9).

a radical centre

One of the most interesting issues around spiritual formation for groups experimenting with models from monastic and religious life is in the area of entry and belonging. There's a widely accepted consensus in western Christianity that Christ-following community needs to be welcoming and accessible. This is coupled with a recognition that even in the recent past the Church has too often been unwelcoming and inaccessible. So in order to encourage more people to follow in the way of the community-restorer Jesus, communities try to be easy to find, simple to enter, and attractive enough to encourage the visitor to stay around.

So far so good. But the monastic tradition seems to lean in a different direction. 'Do not', says Benedict in his rule, 'grant newcomers to the monastic life an easy entry' (*Rule*, ch. 58). Is monastic community different from local church community in this respect? Or is there learning here for all Christ-following community? The root of monastic reticence in this area lies in the lived experience of countless religious that following Christ is actually a costly, demanding path; and that we do the potential disciple no favours by softening the hard lines of this calling. But clearly this is not the whole story. The path may be demanding but it is also a path that shines with hope, possibility and, in the experience of so many monastics, quiet joy. So how is the disciple community to share the full story?

I want to suggest that the aim could be to create community that is radically committed at the core, but easy to access at the edges. This is a demanding balancing act that requires much wisdom and grace, particularly from the highly committed. Benedict himself recognized this tension back in the sixth century, advising in his rule that the abbot of each community should 'so arrange everything that the strong have something to yearn for and the weak nothing to run from' (Fry, p. 88). The shaping of such a community life will need imagination and attention, but my experience is that it is possible for a community with a significant committed core to be able to sustain a larger community of travellers, offering a safe space into which people can come as they are, and continue to make their spiritual journeys.

walk with me

In the monastic community great attention is paid to the novitiate. Following a short preliminary period as a postulant – a period seeking permission to explore life with the monastic order – the potential monk, nun or friar is admitted as a novice. The Community of Bose sees commitment as a process:

> Brother, sister, when you arrive in the community with the desire to follow the Gospel, you do not yet know many things about this life that has attracted you and that you have chosen. You need a period of reflection, during which you can deepen your understanding of the vocation you have received.[1]

This is an extended time in which the applicant lives the life of the community, usually in the particular care of a wise and experienced religious who acts as mentor, guide and teacher. In Benedict's rule a monk is assigned to accompany, not so much to direct but to listen to and to listen with the novice. The period of novitiate is opportunity for both the community and for the applicant to work out if admittance through the taking of vows is the right thing for all concerned. The practice of mentoring is widely receiving new levels of interest and attention at this time, and it seems to me has much to commend it. It's important to see this not primarily as supervision but rather as wise company and sensitive presence. Some of the best mentoring I have received has come through a simple invitation to 'walk with me'.

letting the text work: Lectio Divina

The Christ-following monastic tradition emphasizes engagement with the texts of the faith – principally the New and Old Testaments, but also other great spiritual writings – both through communal engagement in common prayer and worship, and also in individual work. One method for the latter is called Lectio Divina (sacred or holy reading), a process of slowly engaging with the text, allowing it to 'speak', and then to take the reader deeper into union with God. The method has four aspects – *Lectio* (reading), *Meditatio* (meditation), *Oratio* (praying) and

Contemplatio (contemplation). There is often a natural progression through these practices, but they will not always work in such a tidy manner. The contemplatives tell us that the Spirit of God is dynamic and surprising, and we should allow ourselves to fall into the flow of the Spirit's life, rather than impose our idea of what should happen.

It's important to find a way into the practice of Lectio Divina that allows the reader to make the transition from our usual state of activity to a point where we are able to receive. This could be something like the sort of stilling process that this book outlines in Chapter 6, the practice that I call Meister Eckhart's circle.

The sacred reading then begins with *Lectio* – a slow, repeated reading of the text, with an awareness that the text may include a phrase or an idea that is a particular gift for the reader at this time. In *Meditatio* the focus moves more directly to the phrase, idea or thought that has come to the surface in the text. The reader gives attention to this phrase, turning it over, looking at it from different angles, wondering at its meaning, meditating on its particular gift. In *Oratio* the sacred reading moves more directly into what we think of as prayer. Silently repeating the phrase that has come to the fore, we allow it to become our prayer, letting that phrase carry our own deepest prayers and yearnings. Finally, in *Contemplatio* our focus moves beyond our own words and yearnings and on to God, to being in the presence of the Divine, unafraid, joyful, at peace.

Lectio Divina encourages and helps us engage with the vital texts that form the groundwork for Christ-following discipleship and monastic spirituality. I'm also interested in the possibilities of taking the monastic practice of Lectio Divina into unusual settings. St Paul described the scriptures as God-breathed. I am trying to discover what might happen if we paid Lectio Divina attention to the other aspects of existence that we might surmise are also God-breathed, such as the natural world around us, music, mathematics, art or the human person in front of us.

spiritual formation: a practice

I want to suggest a practice of Lectio Divina in everyday life where you are. Try the process first with one of the great texts of the Jesus tradition – that of the Christian monastics who discovered this process – beginning perhaps with one of the Gospels. The Gospel of Matthew is particularly interested in Jesus as teacher, and includes the world-changing Beatitudes. The Gospel of Mark, probably the earliest of the Gospels, takes the reader straight into the Jesus story, and his account is dynamic and sparse. Luke is a brilliant storyteller who particularly loves the stories of the women who were around Jesus. John, probably writing his Gospel after many years of reflection, has a big-picture approach to the story and writes poetically of the importance of the life, death and resurrection of the Christ. Whichever you feel drawn to, stick with it and let the text speak. Give yourself at least 20 minutes a day, and if you can, make it the same time in the same setting each day.

A further development would be to take Lectio Divina out into another area of God-breathed life. Imagine, for example, going for a walk each day in the park near your home. Please note that this practice is not *pantheism* (where in this example God would be the stream, the stream would be God) but *panentheism*, an orthodox Christian belief that signs of God's presence may be found in the created world (the stream carries signs of God's nature and creativity).

You begin by 'reading' what is going on.
This is Lectio.
You observe the trees, the sky, the path and the people.
Is there something here that in God's care
is a particular gift or insight for you today?
Your attention is drawn to the stream running through
    the park.

You walk up to it.

You take in how it looks and sounds, what it does to the
    surrounding air.
This is Meditatio.
You observe the flowing of the stream, the life it seems
    to carry,
but you also see the rubbish that has been thrown into it.
You wonder at what the stream may be showing you.
Why has it caught your attention?

Now you allow your own feelings,
your hopes and dreams,
your frustrations and your anxieties to surface.
You let the sound of the stream become prayer
and allow it to carry your deepest yearnings.
This is Oratio.

Gradually you go into stillness.
This is Contemplatio.
God's presence –
this, you realize, right now,
is all you need.

Ian Adams, 'This is Lectio Divina'

Note

1 Community of Bose website: www.monasterodibose.it 'entering the community'

8

the way of simplicity –
learning from the vow of poverty

For the first time in days
my head is emptied of the
babbling stream of words
blown away
by the wind on the hill
which presses against my lips
the forefinger of hush.

There is a time for speaking
but this is time to be silent.
Words say nothing here.
The wind carries all before it.
And slowly I begin to sense
what cannot be named
only wondered at.

    Ian Adams, 'Blown Away'

For each monk a cowl and tunic will suffice in temperate regions; in winter a
cowl is necessary, in summer a thinner or worn one; also a scapular for work
and footwear – both sandals and shoes. Monks must not complain about the
colour or coarseness of all these articles, but use what is available in the vicin-
ity at a reasonable cost.

    Timothy Fry, *The Rule of St Benedict*, pp. 75–6

towards simplicity

I'm afraid of deep water. I can swim, but perhaps only enough to get out of trouble if I fall into calm water. So sea swimming is always a challenging idea for me. But on a warm day, when the ocean temperature has risen to a reasonable level (perhaps late June after a good early summer here) it seems to evolve from a good idea into something that must be done. My sea-swimming wife happily swims way out. I feel daring just getting out of my depth. But once the initial cold has subsided I love the experience. My fear of drowning meets the grace of salt water, fragility of human form dancing slowly in the immense strength of the ocean. My hyperactive noise is overcome by the sound of the sea. This moment is everything. This is enough.

We live in a world, however, that suggests that we never have enough. The religious life has much to do with helping its participants reach a point where we can say and believe that all our 'this' – what we have, where we are, who we are – is enough. But to learn to live this way requires our immersion in the trustworthiness of existence, our giving of ourselves to the goodness of the cosmos and, as the monastics would encourage us, our free-falling into the goodness of God. A life of 'this is enough' demands that we face our fears of drowning. It requires us to set out into deep water – another wise saying of Jesus (Luke 5.4) – and trust ourselves to what we will find there.

Very early in its life everyone in the small community I belonged to in Oxford decided to try to live for a month without using credit or debit cards. The idea was to simplify our lifestyles, spend less and have a little more in common with the poor in our city. The task was way more difficult than we had imagined. Extricating ourselves, even for a month, from the matrix of interactions, expectations and obligations that we had ac-cumulated proved near to impossible.

Contemporary living involves our compliance with a complex network of interconnections. Some of these connections bring

freedom and release creative energy. There's much about the mul-
tiplicity of ways that humans connect with each other now that is
really energizing. I am writing this on a laptop, connecting with
friends, colleagues and strangers across the world by facebook,
twitter, and email. But it can sometimes feel as if the network of
connections, PINS and information transfer is suffocating us.

In a complex society the religious life appears – at least initially
– to offer a simpler way to live. Often the first thing that strikes
me when I spend time with a monastic community is the sense of
moving towards simplicity. A simple wardrobe – 'for each monk
a cowl and tunic will suffice' – a collective purse, no personal
possessions, a rhythm of life, caring for the poor, a sense of
abundance with less, happiness with the small and a rootedness
to the earth. There is less of almost everything that most of us
surround ourselves with – Fewer words, fewer images, less
stuff – and more of the things that we sense may enhance and
re-imagine the experience of human being – more depth, more
stillness, more reflection.

There is undeniably a movement towards simplicity in the
religious life. But it's really important to realize that for most
monastic communities the religious life is not – and should not be
– a refuge from the world. If we take seriously the pattern of
incarnation given to us in the life, death and resurrection of Jesus,
we have to conclude that a disciple-life needs to be lived within
the wider world, not with our backs turned towards it. The simplicity of the religious life is a gift to our wider communities and
to the places that we inhabit, and it needs to find expression in
that bigger context. Even the closed religious communities live
their simple way in a double movement, seeking the life of God in
seclusion, praying the life of God out into the world.

towards justice

A commitment to poverty in some form is an almost constant
thread running through the practice of the majority of religious

communities. Luke's version of Jesus' disciple-sayings may have been particularly influential. 'Blessed are you' said the teacher 'who are poor, for yours is the kingdom of God' (Luke 6.20). In the best tradition of practising what you preach, the Gospel accounts suggest that Jesus himself practised a life of simplicity.

There are many accounts of Jesus enjoying the hospitality of people he met. Luke tells us in his Gospel that Jesus was supported by his friends, particularly by some affluent women (Luke 8.1–3). And in a scene that suggests something about the humour of Jesus, the travelling rabbi looks to his fishing friends to come up with the coin which will pay the locally levied temple tax (Matthew 17.24–27). The cattle on a thousand hills cannot readily be exchanged for this purpose, and Jesus doesn't seem to carry cash.

Of course there's a difference between being happy with less and grinding poverty. And there's a difference between contentment with a simple way of life for ourselves and doing nothing about the injustices and exclusions that disfigure society. Grinding poverty and injustice are explicitly not what Jesus was advocating. The Gospels look forward to the day when poverty is alleviated and injustice overcome. In Matthew's version of the sayings of Jesus, action on behalf of the exploited is explicitly called for by the rabbi: 'Blessed are those who hunger and thirst for righteousness, for they will be filled' (Matthew 5.6).

Perhaps the best way to understand this teaching of Jesus on the subject of poverty is that he calls us to work for justice for the excluded, combined with contentment with simplicity for ourselves. This is the interpretation of many religious orders, who work to improve the lot of the forgotten people while showing a willingness for themselves to live hidden lives uncluttered by wealth.

How necessary this lived message is at the current stage in the development of human society. Professor Danny Dorling of Sheffield University has shown that in the UK the gap between the poorest and the richest sections of society is continuing to widen (Dorling, *Injustice*). Significant parts of the economy seem to be in the hands of people who make money by moving money, the worst of whose practices seem to have more in common with betting than with investment, fuelled by a dark and addictive cocktail of 'arrogance, ignorance and greed'.[1] Resources, opportunities and wealth seem to remain in the hands of the powerful.

The monastic vow of poverty recognizes that almost all of us might be tempted to operate in the same fashion. So it advocates a better way, and it makes clear that such change must start with us.

simplicity in design

Perhaps it's my northern European background. I favour a minimalist approach in most things. Less is more – now that makes sense to me. I love big expanses of single colours. I like the way that the eye is drawn to simple uncluttered arrangements. I love the music of contemporary minimalist classical composers like Arvo Pärt, John Adams and Philip Glass. And I like the beauty and benefit of simplicity as seen in the design of the Shakers.

This extraordinary religious community of 'ordinary' people emerged in the mid 1770s in Manchester as part of the Quaker movement. Derided and abused as 'Shaking Quakers' because their meetings included singing and dancing, a small group emigrated to North America and settled in Watervliet, New York. The Shakers have become more widely known largely as a result of the simple beauty of design of the products that they made, particularly their furniture. Their designs emerged out of their focus on simplicity and utility, and their rejection of ornamentation. In the process it became clear that simplicity and utility could actually give birth to objects of great beauty. Their designs are full of clarity and strength, graceful curves and clean lines contributing to the usefulness and long-lasting nature of what was produced.

It seems to me that in their concern for simplicity and beauty the Shakers are stepping into an age-old monastic tradition that goes back to the bee-hive cells of the Celtic monks on the island of Skellig Michael off the west coast or Ireland, and even further back to the Desert Fathers. They also ask questions of the monastic tradition. At its usual best the monastic stream lives with simplicity. But occasionally the religious life has lost its way, and a concern for wealth and comfort has overtaken the simple roots of the movement. Some of the monastic houses of the past, perhaps particularly in the medieval period, were very grand indeed. The Cistercian abbeys of Fountains and Rievaulx in North Yorkshire and the Benedictine abbey at Glastonbury eventually included large and magnificent buildings and accumulated huge estates and wealthy commercial interests. Simplicity of life has on occasion given way to less selfless concerns, and it may be that the design of the monastic building and its ornamentation are strong indications of such shifts.

I would argue that at its best the monastic movement has practised and encouraged simplicity in design. However, the really important thing here may not be the adoption or rejection of any particular architectural or design style, but the recognition that design and architecture both reflect and shape our priorities. This can be a virtuous cycle in which our best aspirations in life are reflected in our design, and our simple designs then encourage a deeper simplicity of life.

I love to see architecture that reflects our hopes for a better world now. Design that is bold and accessible, architecture that reflects and complements its surroundings, buildings that connect with and nurture the human spirit. A good example of this kind of architecture might be a building in Dundee in Scotland designed for the cancer charity Maggie's Cancer Caring Centres. The simple curved centrepiece of the building designed by Frank Gehry was inspired by the ancient Highland dwellings known as Brochs. The aim is to create buildings whose design and associated spaces will encourage cancer sufferers, and even help the healing process.[2]

In the spirit of the Celtic monastics, I am also particularly interested in architecture and design that reflect our connection with and our love for the earth.

care for the earth

The earliest desert monastics had learned that nature is a powerful companion, that we belong to the earth, and that if we care for her she will nurture us. So monasteries have almost always been very good at growing things, initially to provide food, drink and clothing for the monastic community, but also for the benefit of the local poor, for visitors and travellers, and for trade with the wider community surrounding the monastic settlement. In his rule, Benedict placed great emphasis on the need for manual labour to provide for the community's needs. 'When (the monks) live by the labour of their hands, as our fathers and the apostles did, then they are really monks' (*Rule*, ch. 48). This was not just about creating the necessary provisions but about the dignity of work and care for the earth. To this day, for many religious communities a key element of their income is produce grown by the community.

Of course, among the wider challenges currently facing humanity, care for the earth is a real and massive issue. The threats to the planet and its creatures by our exploitation, overuse and misuse are well documented. In this context the monastery garden-farm is a resource-full model for us. A community harvesting fruit and vegetables, growing herbs, keeping bees, caring for animals and working with the landscape has much to offer. This kind of undertaking roots a community in its locality, linking it with other producers and consumers and reducing waste.

The friar Francis famously understood the connectedness of all things and celebrated God's great creation. His simple lifestyle,and love for the earth and its creatures has long made him an iconic figure among those who seek to love both God and creation. I want to suggest that in the twenty-first century, any individual and any community that takes seriously our place in the world needs to have a commitment to a simple lifestyle and care for the earth. Inspired by the monastic emphasis on care for the earth, Earth Abbey, based in Bristol, is seeking to encourage a network of new communities committed in God's name to the earth, seeking to 'bring about a peace which embraces all creation'.[3] Earth Abbey's Grow Zones project aims to encourage people to link up locally in groups of between 8 and 20 strong, and to share skills, resources and land in order to grow food, reduce food miles and to care for the earth. At the same time the project inevitably encourages local community to thrive. Some groups are working in community spaces, others in their own gardens. One of the very first things the mayBe community in Oxford did was to dig up some garden and make a vegetable patch, and since then people in the community have started to care for allotments. To care for the earth wherever we are is to step into the monastic stream, involving a literally earthy and essential reorientation of purpose and life, emerging from reflection on the nature of human existence as being inextricably linked to the wider created cosmos.

simplicity: a practice

How can we live more simply where we are? My suggestion here is to make an act of simplification each week. And a good place to start, in the way of the monastics, might be with our clothing.

The religious have generally opted for a simple habit, a minimal wardrobe of simple design and complementary colours that are practical and identifiable. My T-shirt drawer is multi-coloured. There's nothing wrong with that, but the fact is that if I'm to wear clothes that 'go' together (and aesthetically I like that), I need a lot more clothes to make a multi-coloured wardrobe work. That's more cost, more waste, more transport costs and more decisions! Perhaps we could experiment and take a step towards a simpler wardrobe by replacing any existing worn-out clothing with clothes of a similar base colour. Pick your favourite colour and stick with it. Is that boring, or perhaps freeing?

Notes

1 From 'Arrogance, Ignorance and Greed' by Show of Hands 2010: www.showofhands.co.uk

2 www.maggiescentres.org

3 Earth Abbey website: www.earthabbey.com

9

the way of devotion –
learning from the vow of chastity

in step now
we have learned
more or less
to walk together
in time
over two decades more
hundreds of thousands of steps
some slips stumbles
but in step now
and it is good

Ian Adams, 'In Step'

Religion is for lovers
John D. Caputo, *On Religion*

a passionate life

How did it come to this? How did the dynamic way of the passionate, scandalous re-imaginer Jesus give way to so much that is passionless, repressed and safe? How did the movement that challenged an empire become an institution parodied as weak, obsessive or irrelevant? How did the world-turned-upside-down shrivel down into a tired and resigned this-is-as-good-as-it-gets?

At first glance the monastic way might not seem to offer much encouragement in this area. The apparent regimentation of the religious life seems to spring, in part at least, from a deep wariness of human fragility – particularly in the area of our sexuality. The vows of chastity or celibacy, common to almost all traditional monastic and religious communities, might seem to suggest that all that is passionate, particularly our sexuality, needs to be suppressed or controlled. The Desert Fathers seem to have been particularly concerned about the dangers of sexual expression:

> Abba Cyrus of Alexandria was asked about the temptation of fornication, and he replied, 'If you do not think about it, you have no hope, for if you are not thinking about it, you are doing it.'   Ward, p. 118

Think about it, so that you don't do it, is one approach. But perhaps in a more positive direction, many religious are clear in their understanding that their vow of chastity is not just a negative refusal but a positive action, opening up the possibility of a deeper commitment to the Christ. The denial of some aspects of human relationship clears the way for deeper intimacy with the Divine. Some ties are abandoned in order for a stronger connection to reveal itself. The possibility of aloneness is faced in order to discover that we are not alone. The community of Bose make this clear to any seeking to join them in their way of life:

> Brother, sister, the first reality you discover when you enter the community is solitude. Before, you formed your relationships freely and spontaneously; in the community, your ties with people are based only on the same vocation. You have not only given up marriage, you have also accepted the fruitful solitude of the only love, that of Christ.   Rule of Bose 2; 36

And this commitment can be passionate. Sixteenth-century Spanish friar St John of the Cross, founder of the Carmelite order, expressed his devotion to God in terms that seem to stray almost into the erotic, even if expressed to our taste in rather flowery language. With the book Song of Songs from the Jewish scriptures as his foundational text, he imagined his search for God as the secret quest for a lover, conducted under cover of darkness, leading to intimate encounter:

> Dark of the night, my guide,
> fairer by far than dawn when stars grow dim!
> Night that has unified
> the Lover and the Bride,
> transforming the Beloved into him.
>   Marjorie Flower (trans.), *Centred on Love*, p. 10

St John's prayerful quest may give us a glimpse onto a broader understanding of our sexuality – that it can be an expression of a deeper and wider life of devotion.

from chastity to devotion

I want to suggest that at its best the monastic vow of chastity or celibacy is a call to devotion, and the religious life is a passionate call to love – to fall into the love of God, to throw oneself into the love of neighbour and to be immersed in the love of life. This is one reason why I am captivated by the monastic project. There's something compelling about this wholehearted seeking after God, this love, this devotion. Nothing matters more to the religious. Enthused by the possibility of God's presence, suffused by God's love, their quiet devotion is focused in prayer and then flows out into care for the world.

Whatever or whoever the partner in our devotion, the vow of chastity suggests that devotion is best focused, rather than shared indiscriminately. The monastic life demonstrates devotion as being expressed and discovered in deep attention. It looks for the long term, even for the forever, finding ease and stability through a shared life journey. It imagines devotion taking shape in small daily acts of love. And as shown by religious like St John of the

Cross, it suggests that devotion can also flow with passion, wildness and abandon.

The religious life has a long history of mistrust of our sexuality. It has often been seen as something to fear and hence to control and to shut away. So we may be surprised to imagine that the monastic way of devotion, far from repressing our sexuality, opens up the possibility of learning to love and express our sex. It suggests an alternative pattern of relationship that is released and strengthened by devotion, with sex understood and experienced as mutual yearning and intimacy rather than something to be taken, exploited or the cause of shame. Add a little gentle humour to the mix – which the religious I know seem to have in abundance – and this revelation may feel a little like stepping into sunlight. It suggests that our passion and sexuality are part of something much greater, both tasting and bringing about the better world for which we yearn.

It may seem odd to go to a celibate community to find wisdom about love and sex, but in my experience the oddness diminishes when you meet religious and spend time with them. Of course, in the vow of celibacy there may be a sense of loss for some and a toughness to this aspect of the calling for others. But in framing their way of life around devotion towards God they seem to have discovered a beyond-ness, something that our sexuality hints at and points towards, a greater intimacy than even our most abandoned and joyful sex.

Their religion is truly for lovers.

devotion in all of life

In her thoughtful book on 'God, sex and us', Jo Ind asks 'how can we use our sexualities to pursue all that makes for love and joy and peace and justice and everything good that we share together?' (Jo Ind, *Memories of Bliss*, p. 92). It seems to me that the way of devotion can impact for good not just our sexuality and love relationships but how we approach all of life. Devotion can transform our human relationships, our relationship with the divine, even our relationship with the world around us and in which we are earthed.

It offers, to take just one example, a way to begin a new project or role. The way of devotion learned from the monastics suggests that this will need one's full attention. Don't dissipate your energy in many other directions. Avoid rushing, but rather spend time with the project. Let it work away in you. Tell yourself that you are in this for the long haul. Look for ways each day to care for the work. And do every little act with love. Devote yourself.

But like so much that emerges from the monastic way, this is a demanding path and should come with a warning. Devotion is a costly thing in the monastic setting, calling for the making of life-time vows. And it will be a costly thing in everyday life. Devotion to others requires us to know and love ourselves as we really are, and then it calls us to throw in our lot with fellow wounded human beings. The coming together of our shared frailties can be a messy business.

So what might emerge? Perhaps a Christianity that embraces hopeful, passionate and devoted sexuality. And perhaps people of devotion – individuals and communities – characterized by this beautiful attitude in all our relationships. Devoted to the people we love. Devoted to our wider communities. Devoted to justice and peace. Devoted to this amazing planet. Devoted to God.

gazing, being gazed upon

The monastic spirit of devotion suggests another way to understand prayer. What happens to stillness, meditation or contemplation if we see them as an act of love? As a place of potential intimacy? As the setting for divine encounter? Perhaps the greatest discovery of Christian theology, a truth lived out by countless religious down the centuries, is that 'God is love, and those who abide in love abide in God, and God abides in them' (1 John 4.16 NRSV). In their experience this is not a dry academic statement, but the burning light at the centre of all reality, the touchstone for all of life. The Community of Bose recognize this possibility:

> Devote yourself to the art of discerning the divine presence and become a witness to this presence; learn to pray to your Lord without ceasing. Do not value anything above the love of Christ! Christ is also in you, and in prayer you will find his presence in you. If you truly want to live in the presence of God, your prayer should be silent, personal, and hidden, according to the example given to you by Jesus.[1]

One summer a few years ago I ran out of words. I had nothing to say. No prayer would form. Any words I reached for in prayer book or bible seemed written for someone else. In a desolate time this seemed to be one more symptom of my desolation. In time it turned out to be a dark gift, and one of the best things that ever happened to me. I found myself lying on the floor in a foetal position. For days this was all I could do when I tried to enter prayer. After a while, with no end in sight, I began to accept that this might be important, so I decided to let this posture and my silence be my prayer. I could not form words, but I could lie on the floor. I brought an icon of Jesus-as-companion into my prayer space, and I lit a candle. I said nothing. I was coming to realize that I needed to let the desolation do its thing. Gradually, over a period of weeks I had a growing sense that I wasn't alone. No sudden insight, but a feeling that all was well. The ancient Christian contemplative experience of being gazed upon began to take a little shape. I even began to try to return the gaze. Interestingly, I didn't seem to need to rediscover a whole load of words. The gazing was enough.

devotion: a practice

The monastic experience teaches us that devotion doesn't just happen. Devotion occurs in a fluid dance between discovery and making, between surprise and commitment. I want to suggest the creation of a simple pattern of devotion – that of 'being with' someone you love – a close friend, your partner or a family member perhaps.

Make a decision together to devote (that vital, beautiful word) time to being together in the coming week, where you will give each other attention. This could involve conversation, but I suggest that some silence together may prove to be particularly helpful. Do what feels comfortable, perhaps take a walk or get a drink together. Resolve to try truly to hear and see each other. If you are with your partner you may find that this leads into more intense intimacy. There's good precedent for that – Song of Songs, the ancient love song from scripture that inspired the devotional prayer of the friar John of the Cross, is full of intense sexual emotion.

And we imagined that the monastic life was boring?

Note

1 Rule of Bose 2; 36.

10

the way of humility –
learning from the vow of obedience

Lie down
on this hill top
face pressed to
the belly of the world

find yourself
pinned to the spinning earth
intoxicated by the strength of grass
transfixed by the hum of a silent field

filled with ancient sound.
So eat the earth, drink the sky
be held in this mother embrace

     Ian Adams, 'Drunkard's Hill Top'

humility in the landscape

Most days I go out for a walk from the village where we live, set in
a wide valley at the head of a tidal estuary. Through this ritual I am
becoming more aware of each season's character, nuances and
passing. The landscape of this part of South Devon is not on a
grand scale, but understated in its beauty. Flood pastures, land for
crops and fields of grass for grazing animals unfold around
the gently widening river as it curves its way through the valley.
Walking here through the seasons I feel as if I am beginning to
find my place in the landscape. Not so much on it but in it,

occasionally even part of it. No more – and no less – important to the scene than the skylark or swallow in summer, the gull or cormorant in winter.

And I've begun to see that all the best human interventions in the landscape – farmhouses, cattle sheds, fences, hedges, even roads – are those that work in harmony with the land, the sky and the river. They don't seek to dominate the place, but demonstrate a humble desire to be complementary to a landscape that has been evolving long before we came along and which will continue to evolve long after we fold back into the earth. The finest human-designed elements also have a distinctive strength. They don't just disappear but somehow enhance this natural arena with their presence. They highlight this small piece of earth, focusing its shapes, colours and textures in a path, a wall or a roof, that we might better recognize its gift.

'Blessed are the meek, for they shall inherit the earth' (Matthew 5.5), said Jesus the earth-walker and community maker (and possibly house-builder). I find myself wondering how much his own world-view was shaped by his experience of walking in the landscape of Israel-Palestine? It seems to me that in his sayings and stories he shows an instinctive sense of humility, love and companionship to the earth, with wheat and weeds in the mix, paths and fields, walls and houses, birds and foxes. The god-man in tune with his landscape, neither bigger than it nor dwarfed by it.

what to make of obedience?

Perhaps this idea of humility within the landscape is a helpful one in thinking through the emphasis on humility and obedience in monasticism, surely one of the more challenging aspects of the religious life to our contemporary way of thinking.

The emphasis certainly cannot be ignored. The first words of the Prologue to the *Rule of St Benedict* set the tone for what follows:

> Listen carefully, my son, to the master's instructions, and attend
> to them with the ear of your heart ... The labour of obedience
> will bring you back to him from whom you had drifted through
> the sloth of disobedience.   (*Rule*, Prologue, Fry, p. 15)

Benedict goes on to say that 'the first step of humility is un-hesitating obedience, which comes naturally to those who cherish Christ above all' (*Rule*, ch. 5, Fry, p. 29).

This seems out of touch with our current understanding of the way that authority needs to be earned, shared and exercised. But on examining the roots of this emphasis in detail I've come to the conclusion that this is neither an open door to abuse of power nor a call for unthinking obedience. The monastic emphasis seems to be rather about encouraging each monk not to place themselves at the centre of any decision but rather, as Benedict puts it, to 'put aside their own concerns, abandon their own wills' (*Rule*, ch. 5, Fry, pp. 29–30).

This is demanding stuff of course. How many decisions have I made already today that spin out from my (largely unconscious) placing of myself at the centre of my existence? More than a few. My natural inclination is to imagine that life is really all about me, however well I am able to disguise that bias with my attempts to make good decisions that will benefit others. This uncomfortable realization finds echo in the discovery by contemplatives across all faith traditions that it's *not* just about us; that we are somehow connected to each other; and that there is something much wider, more subtle and more interesting going on the universe.

So the focus on obedience in the religious life needs to be seen within the context of creating community. Community depends on its participants. Can we learn to take our place – with hu-mility but also with confidence – in the landscape of community? This is about learning to trust and entrust ourselves to each other. It's about accompanying and being accompanied. It's about count-ing on and being counted on. It's about forging deep connections that will sustain the community.

And so when Benedict's rule calls for sanctions against monks it is invariably because their actions have in some way broken community. They have either intruded too strongly into the landscape of community or demeaned themselves by shrinking back from it – as if buildings have been thrown up without any sense of continuity with what has gone before, ignoring the local materials, with no regard to the contours of the land.

There is undeniably a harshness to discipline in community life in Benedict's rule that we find inappropriate now. But the really vital insight from this aspect of the Rule is that the landscape of community life needs care and attention.

ubuntu and the Holy Trinity

Archbishop Desmond Ṭutu has talked a lot recently about the concept of *ubuntu* – an African understanding of community based on connectedness: 'we are calling from the roof tops that we belong together. We depend upon one another and we can rediscover that essence of shared humanity.'[1] A particular gift of the monastic way is the recognition that shared humanity is born and sustained in humility. Of course, community requires strength and persistence and imagination too, but without shared humility the community project will founder.

The importance of humility has emerged in part from an understanding of the Other that has come out of the religious life of prayer and devotion. Brother Roger of the Taizé community discovered this aspect of the divine nature: 'What is fascinating about God is how humbly he is present. God never punishes, never wounds our human dignity' (Roger, p. 9). How much damage has been done through our ignorance of, or indifference to, this wisdom that has emerged from the monastic life! God, according to the religious who devote themselves to prayer, reveals the God-self gently, over time, in the unspectacular life of attention. The Mystery does not force Mystery upon us. Nor does it submit to our forcing.

A copy of the famous Russian Orthodox icon of the Holy Trinity from the early fifteenth century, written (icons are described as being 'written' rather than 'painted') by Andrei Rublev, is sited on the wall over our meal-sharing table at home. For us it has become a core and essential component in the backdrop to our life. It's unimaginable for it not to be with us, quietly accompanying us in the ordinary-extraordinary wonder of life.

Spend time with the icon, and it slowly reveals some of its surprises. There is a great stillness, but also a strong sense of momentum, the dynamic life of the Holy Trinity. It is, of course, literally silent, but the three figures seem to be in deep conversation, a conversation into which we find ourselves being drawn. The three figures, 'the Sacred Three' of the Celtic tradition, are adult and wise; they are also youthful and even playful. They are male and they are female. They are individual and they are community. They are strong and they are humble. This is the divine nature, understood by the icon-writer Rublev, discovered and lived by the monastics.

It has been said that the answer to everything can be found in Rublev's famous icon. I imagine that if he were here to respond he would point, as the icon always does, beyond the icon, to the reality that it imagines; to the life of God; and to possibility of community which that life inspires and enables.

the gritty business of community life

Community life can be one of the finest of human experiences. It can also be really difficult, even leading to the destruction of the very spirit that we had hoped it would encourage. The monastic way offers practical wisdom to help us cope with the tougher aspects of community, and inspiration to assist us to move towards the finer possibilities of common life.

In the storehouse of monastic experience there is great wisdom for the gritty business of shaping community life, particularly in the areas of participation and leadership. A commitment to participation is one of the key themes of emerging society, and of course monastic life is deeply participative. The religious life is not done to you – you enter it. It's not a second-hand experience.

Benedict's Rule makes some really helpful contributions to the way that a community – indeed perhaps any organization – can take and then hold shape. Monks are recognized for the length of their time commitment to the community, in combination with 'the virtue of their lives, and the decision of the abbot' (*Rule*, ch. 63, Fry p. 85). In this way honour is given to the older members of the community, and their experience is valued, while also stressing that age alone is not enough – much is expected of the older ones in their community-making and life of work and devotion. And Benedict also stresses the importance of hearing other voices. When the community gathers to discuss an issue, he says, make sure that you hear the youngest and newest members of the community, for they will have particularly important insights based on their impressions of community life: 'The Lord often reveals what is better to the younger' (*Rule*, ch. 3, Fry, p. 25). And when your turn comes to make your point express your opinions 'with all humility' (*Rule*, ch. 3, Fry, p. 25).

Regarding leadership, some emerging groups are experimenting with communal leadership. Others, inspired by Benedictine experience, are working with what could be seen as a traditional leadership, but of a very different kind from that modelled by many churches, businesses or organizations. This is from *The Sources of Taizé*:

> As servant of communion, the prior makes his brothers attentive to living a parable of communion together. He should not consider himself above his brothers, but as he fixes the orientations of the community without being bound by a majority, let him seek to understand in God the will of his love.
>
> Roger, p. 55

I wonder what might happen if we were to see this kind of

principle adopted by our leaders in the areas of business, politics and government, as well as in religious community? In the case of the mayBe community in Oxford, these ideas re-worked and reinterpreted have led to a community life with regular all-community conversation, a group of guardians charged with guarding the themes of the community's life, and an abbot or abbess whose demanding task is 'to orientate the community at all times towards Christ'.

humility: a practice

The monastic emphasis on humility and the common vow of obedience can be seen as offering a route into a positive humility, enabling the vow-taker to create vibrant community through humility. This path encourages each participant to learn how to work with the grain of their community, still bringing the distinctive strength, beauty and gift of their own character to the living landscape of community, but enhancing that community through humility, not diminishing it.

I want to suggest that this principle can be taken into almost every area of human activity, encouraging us to learn how to be humble in the context of our own environments while also giving us a pattern for contributing our distinctiveness. Imagine taking this principle into your setting, into your workplace or into your role, letting it shape your studies, your art or your community. When humility and strength are combined – a rare combination – beautiful things emerge.

The practice I want to offer is an exercise in humility that draws on my experience of lying down 'face pressed to the belly of the world'. If you are able to do so, look for a good time and place to lie down somewhere on the ground. Ideally find a stretch of grass, perhaps in a local park or field. Let your senses receive with humility all that is around you. Feel your connection to the earth. Sense that you are held. Enjoy the moment.

Meditate on the great creation story that sees our lifeform first emerging from the earth. Allow yourself to imagine what it will be like one day to fold back into the earth, in God's very good care. My experience is that this is strangely comforting and even hopeful. This lovely old earth seems already to carry signs of its renewing.

This practice is not necessarily only for good weather – I love doing this in the rain in waterproofs and boots. There's something very powerful and humbling about being in the wet grass, rain on your face, sharing the earth's soaking.

The way of humility opens up the path to another monastic secret – the way of rootedness.

Note

1 www.tutufoundationuk.org

11

the way of rootedness –
learning from the vow of stability

To be still
as the heron is
still another glinting rock
in the shallow edge
waters of the shining sea
gazing with intent
content that all will be well
    Ian Adams, 'To be still'

Go, sit in your cell, and your cell will teach you everything.
    Abba Moses, in Ward, *The Sayings of the Desert Fathers*

before you die

Before you die, there are 1,000 experiences to bag, 1,000 books to read, 1,000 pieces of music to hear, 1,000 places to go. Except that you don't have to do any of these things. As good, beautiful or inspirational as they may be – and we really need the good, the beautiful and the inspirational – there may be a better way that is not dependent on these experiences: a path to fulfilment, happiness and truly human-being through engagement with the world as it is, as it finds you, and as you find it, where you are. The monastic way teaches us that there is great value in becoming willing to be shaped by our setting, to root ourselves somewhere specific, to engage with a small piece of the world.

The monastic way of rootedness – the vow of stability in its various forms – calls the monk and nun to find their place of being and to remain there. In the very first chapter of his Rule, Benedict is scathing of 'the monks called gyrovagues, who spend their entire lives drifting from region to region ... Always on the move, they never settle down, and are slaves to their own wills and gross appetites' (*Rule*, ch. 1, Fry p. 21). This is not the disciplined and community-orientated life 'on the road' of the friars. It's a refusal to be committed to people, place or community – in Benedict's view a flagrant misunderstanding and misuse of the religious way.

This call to embrace stability has much to offer us in the twenty-first century. This is not to suggest that we shouldn't travel, or that there aren't seasons when it will be important to be on the road (as illustrated, I hope, in Chapter 5). But it's a recognition that there is great benefit in engaging with the specific part of the amazing green-blue-brown planet on which we find ourselves, rather than always seeking a new experience or a new place. If there's re-imagining to be done it can and must start with me, with us, where we are. In this neighbourhood, this village, this city.

We are perhaps more rootless than most of the generations that have gone before, with many of us disconnected from the land, from our place of belonging and from our people. My sense is that as a result we are also increasingly disconnected from our spiritual roots, from the possibility of the Other. It has often seemed to me that people with a strong sense of belonging to a particular place, perhaps because their family have a long history in that setting, may be in receipt of a special gift. But increasingly for many of us, myself included, our roots and life stories are more complicated. We know where we are, but are not quite sure where we come from. For us the call to find stability and rootedness may be more challenging – but perhaps more hopeful than we can imagine.

places open up slowly

Places open themselves up slowly. They require our presence, our persistence and – that prized monastic element again – our humility. There's a 'tidal road' near our home which runs along-side the estuary. Twice a day the tide covers parts of the road, making it impassable to traffic. If we get the tide times 'wrong' we can end up wading home. It's through walking this road often that I have come to recognize the subtle changes at work in the land-scape. The changes of colour, in wind direction, the taste of the air, the migrating birds. I'm just beginning to recognize the changes that happen when an ebbing tide meets a strengthening wind from the sea. A single fleeting visit to the estuary may be good – it's a lovely setting – but the true gift of the landscape seems to open up only slowly. Perhaps we need time to settle into a place so that we can get out of the way. Our human presence can be so strong, our urge to place ourselves at the centre of the story, that we need to be committed to a place for a long time before our attention finds its true place of being.

The monastic way specializes in preparing the participant for the task of staying with the divine landscape, allowing the life of God to open slowly. In the persistence of the religious life, the daily cycle of prayer and work, rest and re-creation do their quietly apocalyptic (that is, revealing) work, disclosing what truly is. This is why the monastic path is such a patient, long-term quest. And if those of us in 'regular life' commit ourselves to living with quiet persistence and awareness where we are, the most ordinary of human tasks in the most mundane of settings may slowly open themselves up, and be seen to be fecund – pregnant with life, meaning and possibility. 'Getting your bearings' may be a good metaphor for the task of re-rooting of ourselves, for it takes time to see what is around us – both in the physical world and in the wider sphere of God-presence.

discovering wisdom, finding home

The brother who came to the Desert Abba (Father) Moses for wisdom was told simply to go to his cell – his cave – for there he would find all that he sought. The possibility of discovering wisdom for life in an uncomfortably small space might sound strange to those of us who are freedom-lovers. And of course life is more colourful, rich and full when we engage with the wider world – but the point of this monastic teaching is to remind us not to ignore what is right in front of us. The small, the local, the quiet have as much to show us about how to live as the big, the event, the spectacular.

The monastic idea is to find wisdom through stability, by locating oneself in one place. 'This', says the Community of the Resurrection in Mirfield, 'means staying with what is given – something hard to do in a postmodern world ... Over time stability's fruits gradually begin to surprise us.'[1] This sounds appealing, but there are options that clamour for our attention, other enticing fruit. The fruit of relocation can be particularly appealing: change your dwelling place, get a new job, even find a new partner. There may be times when the fruit of movement is clearly the right fruit to pick. When that time comes it needs to be embraced with adventure and hope. Nevertheless, the monastic way always reminds us to consider the option of stability, source of wisdom.

Part of life's wisdom is learning how to come home. The monastic life calls the nun, monk or friar to find a new home in order to discover their true home. The monastic community becomes home to the monk, nun or friar. This may be far from the place of the monk's birth or upbringing – and in my experience many religious communities are comprised of people of many nationalities, for whom their community has become the place of belonging.

So although the roots of our belonging may be (re)discovered in the place of our birth, they are by no means limited to that place. This is good news for those of us who don't really know or sense where we are from. Rootedness and stability are still accessible, however complicated our life journeys. We can find a place to belong and contribute – somewhere to love the people, the creatures and the landscape; somewhere to commit ourselves; somewhere to shape and be shaped.

the place of resurrection

The Christian monks of the Dark or Celtic Age are reputed to have had a belief that relates to rootedness and belonging. A life made new through devotion to God could be discovered and sealed by setting down roots in a new setting, at a site of God's choosing, the 'place of resurrection.' So, for example, there is the wonderful story of the sixth-century monk Brendan 'the Navigator' who sets out from the west coast of Ireland with some fellow monks in a small boat crafted from wood and animal skins, unsure of his destination, but confident alone in God's goodness to bring him to a place of new life, a new world.

There comes a moment in most adventurous enterprises when the early vibrancy of the thing seems to be dying. Everything seems to teeter on the edge of chaos. Failure is close. The death of the project seems certain. All may be lost. This is the moment of crisis. The realization comes that resurrection can only happen through courage, stillness and – the contemplatives might add – love. A prayer attributed to Brendan captures such a moment of crisis, before his journey proper had even begun, with the possibility of resurrection seeming far off: 'Shall I abandon, O King of mysteries, the soft comforts of home? Shall I turn my back on my native land, and turn my face towards the sea?' Any worthwhile venture in life is likely to be costly in some way, demanding much, if not everything, from us at some point. The Dark Age monastic commitment to the place of resurrection may be what we need to sustain us.

finding a thin place

Down some steps into the tunnel. There's a small chapel to one side. I hadn't expected that. Then up some more steps. Out on to the pitch of Barcelona's Nou Camp stadium. The stands tower impossibly tall. I've only seen the stadium on TV before. It's empty today, apart from a few other visitors and ground staff tending the pitch. But to be here is very special. It's not just the sum of its parts, concrete and grass. The Nou Camp carries memories of beautiful games played here. It also conjures up childhood images of me playing football. I'm playing in the yard at school, with dustbins for goalposts. Where did that come from?

George MacLeod, founder of the Iona Community in the 1930s, a resurrection of community life in the spirit and way of the monastics in Scotland, famously described Iona as a 'thin place'. He was trying to put words to his experience of living on the island, discovering that it was somehow a place where the gap that we usually sense between earth and Mystery, between us and Other, between now and Always is somehow diminished. On the thin place of Iona some of the separations present in our experience of existence seem to collapse.

The experience of the monastics provides an insight into the possibility of thin place. I was recently invited to participate in a conversation held by a monastic community who were facing the issue of declining numbers of people coming to commit themselves to the religious life. The discussion focused on how they might respond to this. All options were on the table, including selling up. It soon became clear that among the many reasons that people outside of the community appreciated, even loved, these people was the sense that this was a praying community, and that the place itself had somehow taken on the nature of the prayer made within it. It has a sense of calm, peace and hope.

The place of rootedness may turn out to be a thin place. It may not start out that way. Perhaps Iona was 'just' a beautiful island. Perhaps the Nou Camp was just a playing field. But in time the praying and the playing participated in the coming-into-being of thin place. When we commit to a place, perhaps the same thing will be possible. An emerging religious community might find the pub that it frequents becoming a place where people begin to express their hopes and yearnings, making prayers. An arts project might find its converted studio space beginning to inspire creativity in ways previously unimagined. An ethical trading business might find the generosity and equality of its work spaces triggering off a new desire in others to do things with justice and mercy.

rootedness: a practice

> Stay somewhere.
> Remain in one place.
> For longer than you imagine will be comfortable.
> An hour, a day, a week, a season.
> Stay there for whatever length of time will, you know, be
>   more than you would choose. Give yourself to the place
>   and to the moment.
>
> Ian Adams, 'Stay Somewhere'

Be intuitive about finding this place. The actual location in one sense doesn't matter. It can be rural or urban. It can be well known to you or unexplored. It may be comfortable or perplexing. But find it with care. If you pray, hold the choice of place in your praying. Be open to the idea, in the spirit of those Celtic-age peregrini monks, that the place may find you.

> Picture yourself growing roots into the ground of the place.
> Don't be bashful about belonging here.
> Look people in the eye when you meet.
> Believe that this is your place of wisdom-finding,
> your home-coming,
> your thin place,
> your place of resurrection.
>
> Ian Adams, 'Stay Somewhere'

Note

1 www.mirfieldcommunity.org.uk

12

crossing boundaries – monastic patterns of life and reaching out beyond what we know

I have in mind a mountain
facing the north-west
with humility
and strength
as the weather comes in off the sea

I have in mind a river
unfolding in a valley
with humility
and strength
as the storm-washed stones tumble

I have in mind a small boat
bow-ing into the waves
with humility
and strength
as the harbour light recedes

I have in mind a man
singing his fears
with humility
and strength
as the ocean deepens

I have in mind a woman
praying her losses

with humility
and strength
as she loses sight

of the man
and the boat
the river
and the mountain
   Ian Adams, 'Humility and Strength'

The restoration of the church will surely come only from a new type of monasticism ... I think it is time to gather people together to do this.
   Dietrich Bonhoeffer[1]

discovering charism

The basilica of St Francis and Sacro Convento in the Umbrian town of Assisi is a splendid and beautiful building, the resting place of the friar Francis. It's right that we honour and remember this most influential and inspiring of Christ-followers. It's also probably safe to say that the relative grandeur of this place may not be quite what the friar would have had in mind when he set out on his humble path.

Almost all religious orders have come into being through someone (often just a single person) undergoing a compelling experience of revelation, changing the focus of their life and the shape of its unfolding. The monastic word for this sense of calling and direction is 'charism' (literally 'a gift of grace'). Each religious order treasures its charism. For them it is a gift because it comes from God, and because it gives the community energy, purpose and the ability to persist.

For the Franciscans the charism is summed up in the opening words to the *Rule of St Francis*. There are various versions of the rule, but the meaning is the same, and conveyed here: 'The rule and life of the Minor Brothers is this, namely, to observe the holy

Gospel of our Lord Jesus Christ by living in obedience, without property and in chastity.' The defining themes that emerged in the calling of the life of Francis and in the orders that he initiated were to be a life of poverty in the name, way and spirit of Jesus.

Whenever I work with people who are beginning to think about creating new communities or new projects, I encourage them to begin by focusing on their charism. I don't always call it that, particularly in a non-religious setting – I might refer to it as the 'big idea' or 'the thing you know you must do'. But whatever we call it, my experience is that it is vital to the ongoing life of the venture. This is emphatically not just about the sharing (or in a commercial project, the marketing) of the idea – although this may be important for that purpose. Rather, knowing what you are called to be and to do, sensing your charism, gives you both the necessary strength and humility to persist.

The *strength* of charism is necessary because there will be times when the resulting courage and commitment to the (ad)venture will be all that we have to sustain us. Invariably, everything else falls away at some point – resources, support, understanding and self-confidence. There will be just us, in a small boat bow-ing into a raging sea. And the *humility* that comes from charism is so necessary because there will be moments when even our own strength is not enough. The land from where we set out disappears from view in the storm. We need to draw on the energy and sustenance that comes from beyond ourselves.

This strong beyond-ness may be experienced as the sense that the universe is somehow with us, benevolent, pulling us on, aiding us to see it through, opening up possibility. In the experience of the Christian friars, nuns, monks and, more recently, the 'emergers' inspired by them, that beyond-ness is the mysterious presence of God, the life of what the Dark Age monks knew as the Sacred Three, the Holy Trinity. It's the intuition that the truly good mother-father-God is urging us on. It's the sense that the companion-God is with us in this (in the words of the ancient prayer attributed to St Patrick, 'Christ within me / Christ behind

me / Christ before me / Christ beside me ...). It's the revelation
that the spirit God is guiding us on a path that by turns is full of
joy and surprise. To know your charism is indeed a gift of grace.

flow like water

Water brings life. Water always finds a way. And like water the
various monastic models offer imaginative ways to serve the world
in the spirit and way of Jesus. Whatever field or arena you are
living and working in – business, government, charity, education,
arts, sport, religious or some other area of human activity – there
are dynamic patterns in the monastic way that can be re-
interpreted where you are to help reshape the world for good.

Imagine, for example, what the idea of *cave* might produce in
your context. What might the creation of a 'still place' in your
school or workplace do to the school or work community –
particularly if it is envisioned, planned and created by that
community? What good things might emerge if there is a physical space in the building where people can go to be still, created
and crafted for the purpose by the people who will use it? How
might we enable people to become more self-aware? What
resources might we be able to access to do this? The financial cost
of this will turn out to be well worth the investment.

Or what might taking on the practice of refectory do to you and
to your business or project? Whatever your charism or purpose
(and make sure that you know that), could the offering of hospitality also become a key element in its well-being? How might
this reshape and re-energize our lives? How might the idea of the
refectory change how our visitors, customers, clients or patients
are received – and how might that in turn enable us to bring good
to the local piece of the world that is around us?

And how might the idea of the road contribute to reshaping
your priorities? It's easy and natural to be static. We like what we
know. But perhaps we need to get out more! Are we meeting up
with other individuals, groups or communities in the same field

of work as us? What about meeting up with people working in very different arenas and cultures from our own? What energy and inspiration might that kind of cross-boundary encounter produce? The friar path suggests that it's good to encounter others, to learn from them and to share the gift of our learning with them.

Monastic communities historically have had the freedom and the blessing to work in ways not confined by traditional boundaries on the ground; to flow like water. Their position on what the Franciscan Friar Richard Rohr calls 'the edge of the inside' of the institution means that the religious orders are able to live the life of the Christ beyond the margins of Church life. But their place on the inside means that they also have a place of belonging and a distinct role to help the wider Church discover or recover aspects of its life never embraced or long forgotten. The theologian Dietrich Bonhoeffer recognized the importance of the fluid monastic movement and the wider Church retaining their close connection.

> It is highly significant that the Church was astute enough to find room for the monastic movement, and to prevent it from lapsing into schism. Here on the outer fringe of the Church was a place where the older vision was kept alive.
>
> Bonhoeffer, *The Cost of Discipleship*, p. 46

The monastic movement and the wider Church are both vital if the 'older vision' of a better-world-now as taught by the rabbi Jesus is to continue to be imagined where it seems to have been forgotten, recognized where it is emerging, and brought about where it has been suppressed. The world is no longer static (if it ever was), and our life within it and our engagement with it need to flow like water.

Perhaps a new stream may emerge to do this! A flowing stream of communities, projects, charities and businesses aspiring to live a simple rhythm of life emerging from the wisdom and practice of Jesus. Communities shaped by ancient monastic wisdom and practice, linked to similar communities for mutual encouragement, still committed to the particular denomination or stream of the Church from which they emerged, holding the old traditions close, but improvising new engagement between the good-news story and their setting. Communities in fluid mission of service across boundaries, seen in patterns of engagement that reflect and love the world being engaged with, demonstrating a humble confidence, unphased by the toughness of the times, resisting all attempts at manipulation, with a supple capacity to ride the waves.

the real thing?

The question dominating the opening of the fictional landscape of the TV series *The West Wing* is the search for a presidential candidate who will bring change for good, and do so with authenticity, integrity and imagination. It's the search for someone who might be 'the real thing'. In the UK at least it seems all too often that placing too much hope in any political party, process or promise eventually brings only disappointment and disillusionment. The political priority turns out to be staying in power, rather than doing the good, world-changing thing with that power. And those with power and wealth in other areas seem all too reluctant to share the benefits of their good fortune. I believe that it's vitally important – perhaps more important than ever – to keep on believing in and participating in the political process. And this is emphatically not a suggestion to take on from government, central or local, the services and obligations best done centrally. But there is also a place for other, complementary ways to contribute towards the reshaping of society for good, including politics, *from the underside*. To bring change with authenticity, integrity and imagination.

I want to suggest that new communities inspired by the teaching and life of the Christ, and shaped by monastic spirituality, may be part of this movement. Indeed, they may be uniquely placed to do this. For the monastic life recognizes that the biggest changes will only come about if we change our individual perspective. In the context of community, the religious life reshapes individuals. Change always needs to start with us. In this unspectacular way the world changes.

I like the understanding of the Community of the Resurrection that their charism is something to do with 'sustaining a climate, the climate of God's living presence'.[2] We are familiar, of course, with the idea of preserving eco-systems, the need for us to protect the planet, our obligation to care for the physical environment. The monastic way of life suggests that there is another climate that sustains all of life, essential for all existence. The nurturing, imagining, creating presence of God. This climate – perhaps what Jesus had in mind when he talked about 'the kingdom of God' – is not created by us. It's already there, all around, in and beyond us. The task of religious communities is to keep the rumour of its existence alive, to celebrate the moments when it seems to burst into any and all spheres of human experience, and to allow ourselves to be shaped by this climate, even becoming a breath-full sign of its being (see Dark, *Everyday Apocalypse*).

Through its inspiring of individuals and its commitment to living the climate of God's presence, the traditional monastic life is helping to shape a new flowering of community and mission in the way of Jesus. The religious life generously offers its wisdom, practice and experience in the patterns of cave, refectory and road. May it yield new Christ-following communities, shaped by a rhythm of life, embracing wisdom, pursuing simplicity, living with devotion, characterized by strength and humility.

And so we may see some small signs of a 'real thing' taking shape, bringing good to our world.

crossing boundaries: a practice

Experience someone else's world. Perhaps in the company of friend(s), spend some time in a place that you would not usually visit. Allow any differences to be. Look for common experience.

Make connections. Notice any signs, perhaps unexpected, of that greater but subtle climate of goodness, God's presence. Let this experience work away in you. Talk about it, write about it, make music and art from it, share food and drink through it.

You might like to reflect on how this relates to some of the great stories that the teacher Jesus told – like the parable of the treasure in the field, from Matthew's Gospel. Expect this experience to change you and your community in some important way. With the nun sitting in her cave, with the monk serving in the refectory, with the friar on the road, confident in the company of brother Jesus, there is nothing to fear.

> The kingdom of heaven is like treasure hidden in a field, which someone found and hid; then in his joy he goes and sells all that he has and buys that field. (Matthew 13. 44 NRSV)

Notes

1 In a letter to his brother Karl-Friedrich in January, 1935, in *Testament to Freedom: The Essential Writings of Dietrich Bonhoeffer*, New York: HarperCollins, 1995.

2 www.mirfieldcommunity.org.uk

references and further reading

Bonhoeffer, Dietrich, 1994, *The Cost of Discipleship*, London: SCM.

Caputo, John D., 2001, *On Religion*, London: Routledge.

Colledge OSA, Edmund and Walsh SJ, James (trans.), 1978, *Julian of Norwich: Showings*, Mahwah: Paulist Press.

Dark, David, 2002, *Everyday Apocalypse: The Sacred Revealed in Radiohead, the Simpsons and other Pop Culture Icons*, Grand Rapids: Brazos.

Dillard, Annie, 1985, *Pilgrim at Tinker Creek*, New York: Harper Perennial.

Dorling, Daniel, 2010, *Injustice: Why Social Inequality Exists*, Bristol: Policy Press.

Flower OCD, Marjorie (trans.), 1983, *Centred on Love: The Poems of St John of the Cross*, Varroville NSW: The Carmelite Nuns.

Fry OSB, Timothy (ed.), 1981, *The Rule of St Benedict in English*, Collegeville: Liturgical Press.

Guiver CR, George, *Company of Voices: Daily Prayer and People of God*, London: SPCK.

Ind, Jo, 2003, *Memories of Bliss: God, Sex and Us*, London: SCM.

Laird, Martin, 2006, *Into the Silent land*, London: Darton, Longman & Todd.

Lee, Laurie, 1985, *As I Walked Out One Midsummer Morning*, London: Andre Deutsch.

O'Neal, David (ed.), 1996, *Meister Eckhart, from Whom God Hid Nothing: Sermons, Writings and Sayings*, Boston: New Seeds.

Roger, Brother, 2000, *The Sources of Taizé*, London: Continuum.

Ward SLG, Benedicta (trans.), 1975, *The Sayings of the Desert Fathers, the Alphabetical Collection*, Kalamazoo: Cistercian.

websites

Ian Adams: www.ianadams.info and www.inthebellyofthebig
  fish.blogspot.com
Anglican Cathedral of Second Life: www.slangcath.
  wordpress.com
Earth Abbey: www.earthabbey.com.
i-Church: www.i-church.org
Maggie's Cancer Caring Centres: www.maggiescentres.org
mayBe: www.maybe.org.uk
The Community of the Resurrection: www.mirfieldcom
  munity.org.uk
Morning Bell: www.ianadams.info
Safespace: www.safespace.me.uk
St Egidio: www.santegidio.org
The Community of Bose: www.monasterodibose.it
The Taizé Community: www.taize.fr
The Tutu Foundation: www.tutufoundationuk.org